TRAVEL Writings

Journeying Beyond the Pages

TRAVEL Writings

Journeying Beyond the Pages

Editors

Sarita Chanwaria

Dr. Sarita Jain

AUTHORSPRESS

Worldwide Circulation through Authorspress Global Network
First Published in 2022
by
Authorspress
Q-2A Hauz Khas Enclave, New Delhi-110 016 (India)
Phone: (0) 9818049852
E-mail: authorspressgroup@gmail.com
Website: www.authorspressbooks.com

Travel Writings: Journeying Beyond the Pages
ISBN 978-93-5529-323-7

Printed in India at Thomson Press (India) Limited

Foreword

Desire for Self-Realisations
We travel, some of us forever, to seek other states, other lives, other souls.

Anaïs Nin

Is a prologue to *The Best Women's Travel Writing 2010 True Stories from Around the World* edited by Stephanie Elizondo Grist? In her account, "The Suffer Fest" Mary Caperton Morton says:

> "From around the road's bend: a shriek of metal, a cloud of smoke, and a bus careen at our van, head-on. We swerve madly for a near miss. Then I see the accident: a blue truck in pieces. A man lies in the road, very still. Our van squeals to a stop on the shoulder, and our guide asks if anyone has gloves. We all step out. A crowd has gathered. Somebody has covered the man's face with a bright blue jacket. All I can see is an outstretched hand, lying very still in a pool of darkening blood. I stare hard at the hand, desperately willing it to move, willing it to grab the jacket away, and willing the man to rise. He doesn't. A bystander walks towards us, shaking his head. "There is no suffering here."

As a mountaineer, Morton expands her inner terrain. The *Best Women's Travel Writing* 2010 has a wide range of multitudinous motives that have inspired these adventures. Erika Connor's, *Winter with Street Dogs* narrates her experiences in Rajasthan and empathetically wishes to nurture the street dogs of Rajasthan. Travel writers in the anthology leave homes with a carefully set intention, but eventually, they discover something else entirely.

Travelling has the energy to heal the soul and the potential to renew the zeal for life. It is a fact that travelling is a primordial quest of homo-sapiens. Ever since civilisation's beginning, man has ever been a traveller.

Dr Sarita Chanwaria and Dr Sarita Jain, editor and co-editor of the volume have included a wide range of topics and authors. All the papers and articles are intellectually stimulating. The writers such as Pankaj Mishra's famous travelogue *Butter Chicken in Ludhiana: Travels in Small town India*, Paul Theroux's *The Great Railway Bazaar*, Jhumpa Lahiri's *Unaccustomed Earth* Francois Bernier's *Travels in the Mughal*

Empire and V.S. Naipaul's: *India: A Wounded Civilisation*. There are essays by the contributors such as, *"Travelling: Aspects, Concepts and Philosophy", "The Cambridge Chronicles", "Decoding the Effect of Cultural Dimensions on Global Forms of Travel and Tourism", "Travel Globally with an Open Mind and Heart", "Mystical Inclinations in Journey: A Study of Tagore's Travel Poems"*, and *"Journeying with Frost Through Life"*.

Unlike Christopher Columbus, Vasco De Gama and James Cook who were more of sea voyagers, I would prefer recalling Count Hermann Keyserling, a German philosopher of the early twentieth century, who wrote *The Travel Diary of a Philosopher* which focussed on his method or means of self-realisation or even meditation. Keyserling thought his Travel Diary would not be of interest to people of the present day. At twenty-two, he elected to study philosophy and soon attached himself to that school of thought known as the *Vitalistic* (as opposed to the Mechanistic) theory. The idea of personal perfection is opposed to that of professional efficiency. His journey is the Odyssey of a soul he tells himself:

> "The impulse which drives me into the world is the desire for self-realisation... I am a metaphysician and that means I am interested in the world's potentialities, not in its actualities."

His first long stop is at Ceylon, (presently called Sri Lanka) where he lets his soul vegetate, as do the natives. Keyserling also travels through India, especially the places like Adyar, Bombay, Calcutta, Rangoon, Varanasi, Jaipur, Udaipur, Chittorgarh, Delhi, Amritsar and Lahore. Keyserling visits Annie Besant in Adyar, headquarters of the Theosophical Society. He values Besant and the Theosophists highly because they had revealed the wisdom of the East to the West. In Calcutta, Keyserling visits Rabindranath Tagore, enthralled by their hospitality and the culture, he was a man of rare feelings for perfection in beauty. He even stayed at Shanti Niketan, the Viswa Bharati University and became a lifelong admirer of Tagore's philosophy of liberal education.

Before going on to discuss Amitav Ghosh it is meaningful to consider Aldous Huxley's first essay of *Along the Road*, entitled "Why Not Stay at Home?" which considers using the words 'tourist' and 'traveller' as synonyms; Huxley points out the binary opposition between 'traveller' and 'genuine traveller'. By way of alternative, and somewhat confusingly, 'genuine travellers' are also referred to in this essay as 'travellers born' and 'travellers-for-travelling sake'. Of such "travellers", who in standard anti-tourist discourse are referred to as 'tourists', he writes:

> We call such people travellers because they do not stay at home. But they are not genuine travellers, not travellers born. For they travel not for travelling's sake, but conventions. They set out, nourished on fables and fantastical hopes, to return, whether they avow it or not, disappointed. Their interest in the real and actual being insufficiently lively. It is only the society of their fellow tourists, with whom they conspire, now and then, to make a little oasis of home in the foreign wilderness, coupled with the consciousness of a social duty done, that keeps them even moderately cheerful in the face of the depressing facts of travel.

The "genuine traveller", on the other hand:

> ...is so much interested in real things that he does not find it necessary to believe in fables. He is insatiably curious, he loves what is unfamiliar for the sake of its unfamiliarity, he takes pleasure in every manifestation of beauty [...]

Huxley expands his argument by stating, tongue in cheek, that "[f]or the born traveller, travelling is a besetting vice. Like other vices it is imperious, demanding its victim's time, money, energy and the sacrifice of his comfort". The writer expresses the flip side also in the final paragraph to a subjective, personal statement of Huxley's persona:

> With me, travelling is frankly a vice. The temptation to indulge in it is one which I find almost as hard to resist as the temptation to read promiscuously, omnivorously and without purpose. [...] Deplorable weakness! I try to comfort myself with the hope that even my vices may be of some profit to me.

Huxley's "Why Not Stay at Home" is a fine example of anti-tourist discourse, with its classical, anti-tourist arguments. In the first part of his essay, Huxley carefully distinguishes two different aspects of modern 'cultural' tourism, which clearly show its foundations in the Grand Tour as an ideological project with two 'musts': the refined manners of Paris, and the Arts (as epitomised by Florence, Rome and Venice). In the first part of his essay Huxley mocks modern tourists exactly along these two lines: "Gay Paree" and also Monte Carlo, which represent "Life", while Florence and Rome represent "Art":

> But Paris and Monte Carlo are not the only resorts of pilgrimages. There are also Rome and Florence. There are picture galleries, churches and ruins, and shops and casinos. And the snobbery which decrees that one must like Art – or, to be more accurate, that one should have visited the places where Art is to be seen – is almost as tyrannous as that which bids one visits the places where one can see Life.

The sights in France, Italy, Germany and other Western European countries were visited by the Grand Tourists of the eighteenth century were revisited by the 'Mass Tourists' of the Victorian period. It is one of the hallmarks of this 'Industry' was travel guidebooks (then known as "Hand-books for Travellers"). Huxley's mordacious remarks are relevant and offer a new perspective to read travel writers of the contemporary age.

It is intensely formidable to ignore or avoid Amitav Ghosh as a travel writer. His fascinating books such as *In an Antique Land, Dancing in Cambodia: At Large in Burma* and *The Imam and the Indian* make him a travel writer even though he is wary of labels, he says in *The Imam and the Indian*:

> To those of a taxonomic bent of mind, the contents of this collection may be heterogeneous enough to require classification under several headings. I have resisted the temptation to do this in the belief that connections are of greater importance than disjunctions in the circuitry of the imagination. (*The Imam and the Indian* vii)

Regarding *In an Antique land* Aditya Bhattacharjee in his essay, "The Shadow Lines in Context" points out:

> ...simultaneously an anthropologist's field diary, a historical novel, a detective story, a research monograph . . . a travelogue, a memoir, and...an essay protesting against irrational divisions between people based on ethnicity.

In an Antique Land, a response to his preliminary question, "What happened in this place?" Ghosh, throughout the book, is a man with a mission, correcting Western stories about the region in the course of his south-to-south research tourism. *In an Antique Land,* he expands a footnote by Western scholars into several essays and a book. It is as if since no one else has written about Bomma, the slave, the onus is on an Indian to recover the man from a footnote of history.

Travel writing in the twenty-first century is not merely a literary field it also expands the horizons for cultural studies, contemporary global scenarios, national borders, the geopolitics of the regions, migrations, diaspora identities, constant conflicts of races, ethnicities, gender, class and race, such aspects of human peculiarity and many more are affected by the travel writers in a world of unprecedented global mobility these things need to find a voice.

Pradeep Trikha

Preface

> "Literature and travel are anciently, inevitably tangled, journeys suggest stories, stories take the form of journeys – Odysseys, exoduses, pilgrims' and rakes progresses."
>
> Jonathan Raban

Travel writing or travel literature is an integrative genre, not easily definable as it is multifarious in nature, having different forms and faces conflating elements of personal reportage, autobiography, historical and sociological inquiry and simple story telling or narration and sometimes even much more variegated manifestation like poetry.

Travel is a basic human instinct, coded into our genes from an evolutionary past, when migration was an essential form of survival. Today, when our lives do not necessarily depend on setting out in search of greener pastures or happier hunting grounds, the purpose of travel has become more nuanced and varied. Be it quest for knowledge, spirit of adventure, propagation of knowledge, pilgrimage, earning of bread or simple wander-lust, all have prompted and promoted man to travel.

Travel literature covers every inch and instinct of human life and human thought. Its horizon spreads from earth to space – from the highest mountains to the deepest oceans, from pilgrim places to historical destinations, expressing and delineating great artistic skills and vivid descriptions of the travelers.

Travel has been a major theme of literature and we have a long tradition of travel literature across the world. Travel writing reveals the concealed facets of human life. It celebrates the strange, exotic and foreign aspects of people and places and their manners and cultures, worldwide and harmonizes the differences into the string of ecumenical.

> "The Wish to travel seems to me characteristically human: the desire to move, to satisfy your curiosity or ease your fears, to change the circumstances of your life, to be a stranger, to make a friend, to experience an exotic landscape, to risk the unknown."
>
> Paul Theroux

Travel writing broadens our perspective and makes open our hearts and minds. It promotes globalisation and multiculturalism and brings the world and humanity a little closer. All the places worth visiting that remains unexplored, every nook and corner of the land has been trodden and has become a source of impassionate curiosity and educative value.

> "The travel writer seeks the world we have lost – the lost valleys of the imagination."
>
> Alexander Cockburn

The paper Journey towards 'Self': Chasing the Travelling Women in Rani Padmini by KarthikaV.P. Is an attempt to follow the travelling women Rani and Padmini in the Malayalam movie *Rani Padding* and to observe and analyse their quest and conquest to add a new meaning to their lives? This paper beautifully showcases that how travel is used in the movie not just as a movement from one place to another, but also as a movement from the 'self' created by the society to the 'true self'. Dr. Sanjana Sharma in her paper *Metamorphosis of Self through Journeys: A Discourse upon the Autobiography of Krishna Hutheesing* aims to highlight the impact of travelling on the life and personality of Krishna Hutheesing as portrayed in her life narrative *With No Regrets: An Autobiography* as formation of the self is imperceptibly affected by geographical and temporal conditions of one's life. An individual's identity is developed over time, constantly evolving, and influenced by self-awareness. Ambika Gahlot and Anant Pandey in their paper *Travelling: Aspects, Concepts and Philosophy* have tried to discuss in detail different dimensions and aspects of travelling by taking into consideration examples from our daily lives along with literary texts. The concept of travelling is as old as our civilisation. The traces of human travelling for miles can be dated back to the primitive ages when even the concept of means of transport was alien to us.

Dr. Urvashi Sabu's personal memoir *The Cambridge Chronicles*, a vignette from her unpublished daily journal describe a days' visit to the university town of Cambridge with Duncan Large, the academic director of the BCLT, UEA, Norwich UK. Also, that how her vision expanded and perception of the self and the other has turned upside down. Anita Luther Bhasin's paper *Children of America: Narrating the Transnational Experience in Jhumpa Lahiri's Unaccustomed Earth* explores the inter-generational clashes. In dealing with the metaphoric striking of roots deep into American soil, the stories go on to briefly delineate the struggles and process of acculturation of the parents and the easier integration of the children who embrace American values of individualism and freedom of choice in matters of love, marriage and careers. *Searching for Self in V. S. Naipaul's India: A Wounded Civilisation* a paper by Anoopama Yadav posits a new individuality that confers boundaries and limits and brings into relation various temporal and spatial metaphors. While entailing about India, the land of his ancestors, Naipaul projects his wounded feelings and bitter realisation of his roots. In this paper, the selfhood of displaced Naipaul is seen in the context of cultural identity theory postulated by Stuart Hall.

Anshuman Singh Chauhan in his paper entitled *Decoding the Effect of cultural Dimensions on Global Forms of Travel and Tourism* focus on the dynamics of Geert Hofstede's Cultural Dimensions. The paper aims to establish a casual connect among basic six dimensions, presented by Hofstede, and their effect on mindset, social cultural systems and perspectives of people hailing from different countries. Mamta Chanwaria's paper *Mystical Inclinations in Journey: A Study of Tagore's Travel Poems* seeks to trace the poet's prophetic vision, spiritual wistfulness, and ecological wisdom, oneness with nature and mystical inclinations in his poetry and make travel an infinite experience for his reader. Tagore's vision and his experience is well expressed through his poetic thought and this piece of writing is a sincere effort to probe into, to move with and to procure the different shades and aspects of journey through his colloquial and natural verses. Dr. Rashmi Bhatnagar in her paper *A Kaleidoscopic view of Paul Theroux's The Great Railway Bazaar* describes an entertaining and exhaustive railway Odyssey undertaken in 1973. It's a grand journey beginning from Europe in the Direct Orient Express which links Europe to Asia. The book portrays not only the outer atmosphere, scenes and pictures but also the interactive episodes of fascinated men he meets in the journey.

Dr. Atiqa Kelsy in her paper *journeying with Frost Through Life* deals withsome of Frost's poems that use travel, journey as a constant symbol of life that goes in and as it goes on, people learn, people grow and pick up lessons on the way as they go ahead in their journey of life. Robert Frost is known for using symbols to express the practical wisdom of a farmer but also elevating that local wisdom to the universal level. Among those symbols, traveling or journeying forms an important part of Frost's oeuvre. Mrs. Anita John in her article entitled *Travel Globally with an Open Mind and Heart* endeavors to bring forth the myriad ways in which travel changes and expands our repertoire of social, emotional and physical well-being. While doing so, it draws upon the author's personal experiences, weaving travel vignettes with the profound life lessons acquired during her travels. *Bernier's Travels in the Mughal Empire: A Socio-Religious Perspective* a paper by Dr. Prerna Maheshwari make allusions to Francois Bernier's observations on the socio-religious conditions in India. Bernier was a French traveler, historian, political philosopher and physician who visited India in the 17th Century. This paper makes an assessment of Francois Bernier's travel account in relation to its cultural relevance that helps to understand the European perspective on India in Mughal times.

Narrating Modernity and Globalisation in Small Indian Towns: A Study of Pankaj Mishra's travelogue Butter Chicken in Ludhiana a paper by Dr. Kirandeep deals with fascinating travel book Butter Chicken in Ludhiana: Travels in Small town India (1995) by famous Indian novelist and essayist Pankaj Mishra. It is an earnest effort for mapping the intellectual crossroads where the dynamics of globalisation have joined the forces of modernisation in inducing social change in India. Guman Singh Gehlot's paper Pilgrimage as a medium of portrayal of society: An analysis of Chaucer's The Prologue to the Canterbury Tales employs the idea of pilgrimage to portray the character of contemporary society. He brings together people from different walks of life ranging from the sacred to the secular, and the profane. The characters are timeless and temporal. Chaucer, with the help of irony and juxtaposition suggests the hollowness and hypocrisy of contemporary times which can be identified in modern society too. Marlowe as the Narrator in the Heart of Darkness: As Agent of Civilisation and Against Primitivism a paper by Dr. Ranjit Kaur attempts to discuss the aspect of Marlow's whimsical indirection, fragmentation, hesitancy, and the like, tend to increase as he proceeds up the river and focuses on how Marlow assumes a middle-of-the-road position on everything and seeks to mediate between the extremes; in this, he embodies the British spirit of compromise.

Dr. Gargi Singh in her article *Cognitive Perspective in Sculpting Travel Memories* discusses in detail the cognitive aspects of sculpting travel related memories. Long-term memory and predominantly the role of episodic memory and its functional aspects in retrieving travel memories from experiences are dealt with efficiently. The insights in this article are inspired by personal experiences wherein an attempt has been made to draw connections with the social aspects as stimulants to thinking and generating memories. *Illusion versus Reality in An Area of Darkness by V. S. Naipaul* a paper by Dr. Yashoda Verma depicts the diasporic dimensions of Naipaul's life experiences. In this novel Naipaul portrays India as a "dark area." Its central themes are alienation and solitude. It chronicles his failed attempt to settle in India. Dr. Tanuja Yadav in her paper *Narrative of Quest for Spirituality and Emergence of Self in Yolande's India, India* explores the journey of Yolande Villemaire, a Quebec writer, to India. Her sense of belonging to her roots in Quebec, Canada is expressed through her description of the people, culture, and places of India.

Dr. Jyoti Sareen in her paper *Seize the Day: Zindagi Na Milegi Dobara* explores the inseparable association of the story with its setting and establishes how the location complements the narrative "unfolding the interrelations between lived experience and a more abstract or unpresentable spatial net-work that subtly or directly shapes it" through analysing the movie *Zindigi Na Milegi Dobara. My Trip to Maheshwar: A Memoir* a paper by Dr.Mamta Chanwaria explores the beautiful ambience of a lesser known and less crowded place Maheshwar a small town situated on the banks of Narbada river in Khargone district of Madhya Pradesh, around ninety kilometers from Indore. In this chronicle the author shares her experiences of two day trip which was full of immense blissful moments, divine grace, varied experiences, learning, exploring, sightseeing and of course relaxing for some leisurely hours. Dr. Alka Jhajharia in her paper *Understanding Travel Writing as an Act of Cultural Translation with reference to the Travel Narrative of Nancy Prince* focuses on the idea of 'cultural translation' as described by Bhabha with special reference to the travel narrative of a black woman writer. The narratives by black women demonstrate the tension involved in forms of difference between race and gender. The paper mainly refers to the autobiographical work of a black woman.

This book will take the readers on a journey beyond the pages, opening up new vistas for further exploration; to new places, new cultures, new people, and a step forward towards new knowledge and experience.

> "If you can't travel, read. Reading is like travel, allowing you to exit your own life for a bit, and to come back with a renewed, even inspired, perspective."

Laurie A. Helgoe

We cannot conclude this prefatory note without expressing our gratitude to Dr. Pradeep Trikha, Associate Dean, UCSS&H & Professor, Department of English, Mohan Lal Sukhadia University, Udaipur (Rajasthan) currently Visiting Professor, Department of British Studies University of Munster, Germany for writing the 'Foreword' for the book. Our sincere thanks are also due to the Authorspress for their unflinching support in printing the book so beautifully.

Sarita Chanwaria

Sarita Jain

Contents

CHAPTER 1

Journey Towards "Self": Chasing the Travelling Women in *Rani Padmini*

Karthika V. P.

Abstract

It is a known and accepted fact that, the most pertinent thing that enabled the human civilisation to flourish and perpetuate as we see it today is the human being's irresistible tendency to seek, to move, to explore, to discover and cross new frontiers and to familiarise themselves with the new environments. Travel is an inevitable part of human civilisation. When a person travels, he/she moves from one place to a new place which is different from his/her home environment. This difference can have great impact even on the identity as it may bring a sea change in their perspective and ideas.

In recent times, travel in narratives, has arrested the attention of researchers and critics. Authors and film makers have used travel as a motif to elicit various experiences. In many of the narratives, the auteurs have juxtaposed physical description of the journey with the psychological odyssey of the protagonist. Prior to the twentieth century, the travel writing portrayed the travel experiences of men. Women were the "patient Penelopes" who waited at home for their partners. But in recent times, the attitude has changed and women's travel writing and experiences have also become a topic of serious study In this paper, my attempt is to follow the travelling women 'Rani and Padmini, in the Malayalam movie *Rani Padmini* and to observe their quest and conquest to add a new meaning to their lives. Through the close analysis of the movie, the attempt is to show case how travel is used in the movie not just as a movement from one place to another, but also as a movement from the 'self' created by the society to the 'true self'.

Keywords: Journey, explore, life, Rani Padmini, self, quest.

Rani Padmini is a Malayalam Film released in 2015, directed by Ashiq Abu. The film depicts the journey of two women who came from entirely different backgrounds and their interpersonal relationship which helped them to complete their quest to identify themselves.

The film was scripted by Syam Pushkaran and Ravishankar. The role of Rani and Padmini were donned by Rima Kallingal and Manju Warrier respectively. The film received wide critical acclaim as it portrayed the journey of two women travellers, which was a comparatively new subject as far as Malayalam cinema is concerned.

The film opens with a song which juxtaposes the childhood of two girls Rani and Padmini. The song unveils that one girl (Padmini) is born into a traditional family in a rural village of Kerala and her father is a renowned Vaidya (Ayurveda Acharya) and she had been brought up in a way inculcating her interest in ayurvedic medicines and treatment. She had been brought up in a way conforming to the traditional societal notions about the upbringing of a girl child. And she also grew up accepting the role designed by the society. The other girl (Rani) was born into a middle class family and was grown up as a tomboyish girl, not conforming to the traditional role set up of the society. She was a troublemaker and a constant headache to her mother. The film follows a non-linear narrative pattern.

The next scene shows the grown up Padmini contemplating on her decision to travel alone. She is worried about her social status, her father's status and wonders what people will say if Sankaranvaidyan's daughter sets out for a solo journey. Her dilemma in taking this decision is the portrayal of the reality which prevents most of the girls from dropping their dream to explore the world. Here, Padmini has a reason to start this journey or rather a strong reason which compelled her to set out for her journey. On the way towards her destination, she meets Rani, who also travels for a reason and both of them develop a strong bonding and help each other in solving their personal problems The reasons behind their decision to travel is unveiled during the course of their journey.

Padmini, as mentioned above, was brought up in the traditional way. When she grew up, she gets a marriage proposal from a Delhi settled Malayali family. The marriage got fixed, and the boy's mother who was very authoritative asserted that the reason why they fixed the marriage was because, they found it out that Padmini was a girl with "adakaumothukaum"(a girl who conforms to the societal rules regarding the behaviour/ upbringing of a girl). The mother also said that in fact she needed a companion more than her son. However, everyone including Padmini was happy with the proposal and she got married to Giri who is a car rallyist. After marriage she moved to Delhi and she went there with lot of dreams, like to visit

Qutubminar, explore the city etc. Her husband loved her, treated her well, however, he was a bit indifferent and completely gave everything upon the decision of his mother.

Padmini adjusted with her new life and took care of all the household thing, supervised the functioning of the farm that her mother-in law owns and acted according to the decision of her mother in law. Her husband was fond of cars and car rallying and showed least concern for the dreams of Padmini. He was not an abusive or chauvinist husband, but the only thing was he ignored or failed to understand the his wife also had some dreams and passions. Two years after their marriage, one day, during their breakfast time, Padmini garnered strength and asked everyone the permission to join a nearby hospital as a physiotherapist. The mother in law reciprocated to it sarcastically, but later on her husband gave her confidence by saying that if she wished to do something, she has to go for it, as he never sought anybody's permission to do things that he wished to do. This motivated her and she joined the hospital. One day when her husband left for Manali for the Great Himalayan Car Rally, her mother in law told her that she wanted a daughter in law who could assist her fulltime and not part time. When she gave a cold response, her mother in law showed her the joint divorce petition signed by her husband and gave her two options, either to sign on the divorce petition or else to resign the job. She got startled to know that it had been signed by her husband. She wanted to talk to her husband to know the reason which prompted him to sign the paper. She knew well that he loved her, and he must have signed it under pressure. However she wanted to confirm it and then she takes a decision to travel to Manali to meet her husband. Being born into a traditional family, the decision to travel alone was something which is nonconforming to the ways in which she had been brought up. But then she comes to the realisation that while travelling a girl can come across only that much danger which can come up to her even if she is at home. With that realisation she decides to start her journey. She takes her ornaments and some money and sets out for the trip to Manali.

In the bus, she meets Rani. Rani was staying with her mother and grandmother in a flat which was under the threat of confiscation by bank. Rani was the sole-breadwinner of the family who was trying her best to tackle the financial issues. However, she was short tempered, tomboyish and hated the fact that no matter how much she struggles to make both ends meet, her mother cribs for the fact that she didn't have a son. One day, because of her anger issue, she gets sacked from her job. One day she happens to notice that her new neighbour is a notorious drug pedlar wanted by the police. And the police has announced 15 lakhs reward money to people who give information about this goon. Rani informs the police about the goon, however, the goon was so influential that he gets to know about Rani from the Police itself. He comes and tries to attack Rani and demands for money. Rani fights back and meanwhile, the goon get a very bad spinal sprain which leaves him under constant and severe pain. So Rani decides to run away from Delhi to escape from this goon and his sidekicks.

During the course of journey Padmini who is a very naïve girl with very little travel exposure tries to befriend Rani when she comes to know that Rani is also a Malayali. Rani shows her arrogance in the beginning. Padmini suffers from motion sickness, gets tired and tells Rani her problems and requests her to somehow help her in reaching her husband. Rani, even though irritated agrees and they reach Manali. They get to know that the goon and his associates have also reached Manali in search for her. They flee from there, and somehow they manage to reach the camping place of the rallyists. Padmini's husband's friend sees Padmini and as he doesn't want to distract her husband's attention, he decides to trap her and send her back to Delhi with the police. He tells them to stay there for a night as she will be able to meet her husband only the next day. So thinking that Padmini's problem will be solved soon, Rani takes the gold and money from Padmini and leaves the place. When Padmini wakes up, she reads the letter from Rani, telling her that as her problem is solved, she is taking money to solve her own problems and also asks Padmini to be like a fighter. Padmini gets angry and she follows Rani, finally confronts her and both of them fight. Padmini becomes unconscious. With the help of some trekkers Rani hospitalises Padmini and both of them feel sorry for what had happened. They sort out the problem between them and Rani tells Padmini that the trekkers will help them to reach Leh through a shortcut. So they start their journey with the trekkers.

The trekking opens a new avenue before Rani and Padmini. They begin to experience the real meaning of freedom. Padmini realises that the tagline of a girl with 'adakkam and othukkam' is actually a chain that is used by the society to prevent a girl from exploring and experiencing freedom. Rani also understands that one doesn't have to be a boy to enjoy real happiness. It is an awesome experience to be a woman. One has to open one's eyes and mind, enjoy the reality and nature, and then you can experience the real happiness. Rani helps Padmini in reaching out to her husband and Padmini, uses her physiotherapy skill to correct the spinal sprain of the goon and there by saves Rani from the goon. The problems are tackled and movie ends on a happy note.

In this movie, we can see that the journey of these two women is a journey of self-discovery and revision of their roles and position in the society. Here journey is presented as an escape from their normal life. While travelling only, they realised the meaning and purpose of their life. Padmini who used to complain about her husband's obsession towards car rallying and who used to ask him the reason for his interest in rallying now realises thatno solid reasons are required to follow the passions. If you have passion, listen to your inner voice and follow the passion and that will make you happy. The journey offers realisation not just to Padmini, but also to Giri, her husband who realises the love of his wife and the love he has for his wife.

The journey also prompts them to explore their psyche to find their true selves. Earlier, Rani was searching for job. One day one art director gave his card as he found her eyes beautiful and wanted to use it for an advertisement. Then Rani neglected the offer. But later on she finds her potential and accepts the offer and becomes successful in that. The movie also highlights on the female bonding which developed during the journey. Rani and Padmini, though they are of two different natures, from two different backgrounds develop a strong bonding. In most of the Malayalam films, even if women travellers are portrayed, there would be an accompaniment of a male companion. Moreover in such cases the focus will be to highlight the valour and resourcefulness of the male companion and how he protects the female protagonist from the adverse happenings during the journey. However, in this film we can observe a deviation from the cliché portrayal of women travellers in the Malayalam movies.

References

Abu, Aashiq, director. *Rani Padmini*, Fort Entertainment, Oct. 2015, www.youtube.com/watch?v=rCr_EE32Ld4.

Dispenza, Joseph. The Way of the Traveller: Making Every Trip a Journey of Self-discovery. Emeryville, CA: Avalon Travel Pub., 2002.

Jonathan Raban, For Love & Money: Writing – Reading – Travelling 1968-1987. Picador, 1988, 253.

Wikipedia contributors. "Rani Padmini (film)." *Wikipedia, The Free Encyclopedia.* Wikipedia, The Free Encyclopedia, 9 Jul. 2021. Web. 7 Sep. 2021

CHAPTER 2

Metamorphosis of Self through Journeys: A Discourse upon the Autobiography of Krishna Hutheesing

Dr. Sanjana Sharma

Abstract

The philosophy of self seeks to describe essential qualities that constitute a person's uniqueness or essential being. The self can be considered as the source of consciousness, which is responsible for an individual's thoughts and actions. One essential difference between human beings and other creatures is to be found in the structure of a human being's will. Present paper tries to analyse the formative influence of sojourn on the identity of Krishna Hutheesing as delineated in her life narrative entitled *With No Regrets: An Autobiography*.

Keywords: Autobiography, self, identity, psychology, persona.

Self-concept is the way people think about themselves. It is unique, dynamic, and always evolving. This mental image of oneself influences a person's identity, self-esteem, body image, and role in society. The formation of the self is imperceptibly affected by geographical and temporal conditions of one's life. Edward Soja, a noted postmodern geographer and theorist states that the geographical locations have a formative influence on self-awareness. He says that people's life stories have geography too; they have milieux, immediate locales, provocative emplacements that affect thought and action (Soja 139).

Every human being is unique in mind and in body, in feeling and intuition. Eminent scholar and critic Prof. Jasbir Jain expressing views on the relations between self and autobiography observes: "autobiography is a framing of the self by the self and is always in process" (Jain 64). By writing an autobiography, a woman reveals her distinctive self and indulges in self-exploration. Krishna Hutheesing has written her life's narrative entitled *With No Regrets: An Autobiography* that is unique in itself.

An individual's identity is developed over time, constantly evolving, and influenced by self-awareness. When a person goes through one's memory and experiences, and organises them through a careful selection, one gives shape and form to the indefinable and fluid self. There have been different approaches to explore self within Indian philosophical, religious and spiritual traditions. The Vedic approach was dynamic with focus on things outside the self-such as rituals, as it celebrated one's relationship with nature, cosmos, earth, sky, etc. The Upanishad approach was inward and introspective. Adi Shankara, also known as Adi Shankaracharya, was an eminent Hindu saint and philosopher. He held that the very essence of the self is chaitanya, or pure and unadulterated consciousness.

Karl Weintraub's epoch-making work *The Value of the Individual: Self and Circumstance in Autobiography* (1978) traces the history of the self by focusing on key autobiographies stretching from past to the present day. William Spengemann's *The Forms of Autobiography: Episodes in the History of a Literary Genre* (1980) identifies three forms of autobiography, the 'historic', 'philosophic' and 'poetic'. Charles Taylor's *Sources of the Self: the Making of the Modern Identity*, (1989) discusses many of the canonical autobiographical texts to illustrate the development of the modern self.

Edward Hoffman, *adjunct* clinical associate professor of psychology at Yeshiva University in New York City states that travel specifically helps with problem-solving and decision-making (Hoffman). The travel theme in the autobiography of Krishna Hutheesing has a kind of orientation that enables her to seek and establish her own identity. Travel plays an important part in educating a person and leaves one with indelible impressions. As the narrative advances, the reader travels along with Krishna and watches how the personality of the writer undergoes a sea change during the various sojourns. She narrates that when the annual session of Congress was held in Ahmadabad, Gandhi asked the Nehru women to attend it in the absence of Motilal Nehru and Jawaharlal Nehru who were is prison then. For the first time in her life Krishna travelled through the third class of the train and found that journey was far from being comfortable. However, she harbored great patriotic feelings in her heart and thought that this experience was an education in itself and for the first time she realised how deep rooted was the faith and affection that the masses had for Gandhi and other congress leaders. She has engagingly delineated love and devotion of the common people for these travelers, "At every station, no matter how late or how early the hour, large crowds surrounded our compartment. They flooded us with flowers and food and tried to show in hundred simple ways that they appreciated the sacrifices that the leaders were making to win Swaraj for the people" (37).

Along with other members of the family Krishna had to stay at the Sabarmati Ashram in Ahmadabad. Rooms were bare and not too comfortable. There she would wake up at 4 a.m. to attend prayers. She had to do washing for herself and was served simply boiled food without ingredients in it. She confesses truthfully, 'I for one was perpetually hungry and looked forward to going home and having a square meal. (38) She found that it was no joke washing the thick *khadi*. Living at ashram and being able to see quite a lot of Bapu was a grand experience for her.

Todd B. Kashdan, a professor of psychology and a senior scientist at the Center for the Advancement of Well-Being at George Mason University, in an article entitled "The Mental Benefits of Vacationing Somewhere New" believes that travel should routinely be used to achieve the opposite: to get out of your comfort zone, expose yourself to uncertainty, and eschew rest for exploration and learning. The result is personal growth, greater emotional agility, empathy, and creativity (Kashdan). Krishna Hutheesing's visit to Europe in the year 1926 has consequential and far-reaching impact on Krishna's temperament and persona when she goes all alone to Europe, unchaperoned for the first time in her life. Most of her family members were already in Europe and she was to accompany her father. Due to some important court case hearing, he could not go along with her. She was both a little afraid and excited at the prospect of the new life before her. She had never been away from home without her family nor had travelled alone but she knew very well that if she missed this chance, she might not get another chance in near future. Therefore, she decided to go, and states in her autobiography that it was a wise decision (42). Her mother was most distressed and annoyed at her father for having allowed her to decide on such a step herself. She thought it highly improper for a young woman to travel all alone to a strange country and tried to dissuade Krishna from going. After having boarded the ship, whenever Krishna talks to a young man, she is lectured by some friends, who take it upon themselves to act as her guardians. She is advised to not to became friendly with any strange man. On the stroke of ten, she has to go to bed every night. She submits to this programme for a few days but later she rebels. She is bold enough to put up with more sermons and dark looks, which she survives unscathed.

On her visit to Europe, she first visits Rome and Florence and feels thrilled. During this tour, she finds in Jawahar an ideal companion and a most delightful guide. The flat in Geneva was a small one and she missed the large rooms and spacious grounds of Anand Bhawan, her home in Allahabad. She starts learning French anew and she has to do house-keeping, as her sister in law kamala Nehru is ill. She manages both tasks skillfully.

Along with her brother Jawahar she attends International Summer School in Geneva which is also attended by several other Indians, Chinese, Ceylonese, Americans, French and Germans. There the lectures are given by well-known statesmen, professors from Oxford, Cambridge, and by some famous authors as well. During weekends, the school organised excursions and she and Jawahar often attended them. She remembers how Jawahar managed a narrow escape on a mountaineering expedition and how she seemed to die a million times in those few seconds.

The visit was a turning point in Krishana's life as it gave her a chance to meet the great stalwarts of the world. Accompanied by her brother she visits Romain Rolland who lived at Villeneuve. She met Einstein when he was present at a lecture given by Sir J.C. Bose. She also had a chance to meet great poet Ernst Toller in Brussels who was a victim of the Nazi regime. His two great passions were truth and devotion to the cause of freedom. She also goes to the hill station called Montana. Here she takes part in winter sports for the first time in her life. She learns to ski and skate and is fascinated by the skiing at which she spends many delightful hours. During their stay at Montana, she and Jawahar take trips to every now and again to France, Belgium, Germany and England and she loves Paris specially.

Her brother Jawaharlal Nehru attends various conferences in Europe and offers to take her if could be useful and act as his secretary. She is thrilled at the prospect of going with him but feels a little dismayed at acting as a secretary as Jawaharlal is a hard taskmaster and does not stand inefficiency. However, she finds the offer tempting and she straight away borrows his typewriter and sets to work on it to equip herself for future. From then onwards she accompanies him on almost all trips. She thinks that going with Jawahar on such trips was quite an education in itself but not always as much fun as she had thought it would be. Jawahar never spared her for he thought hard work was always good for one and according to him, Krishana had never done any before-"He said I had too easy an existence and a little roughing would improve me enormously. I am sure it did…" (47).

She visited various museums and art galleries with her brother in Europe. When she felt tired and suggested to hire a taxi, Jawahar would consent on condition that they should give up the idea of going to the theatre that night. For Jawahar too much luxury all at once was very bad for one and sullenly she would give in. She admits that it proved a wonderful training for real life and she could never have gone through such thing here in India. Nevertheless, she confesses that at that time she almost hated her brother for inflicting what she thought were unnecessary hardships on her.

In early 1927, the League against Imperialism was held in Brussels. Krishna went to attend it along with Jawaharlal. It shows her undaunted courage and the undiminished desire for the cause of freedom. Remembering the friends of different nationality she made during this European tour, she grieves that she has lost their trace as Nazi hordes swept over their countries. She often wonders where they are now, whether in concentration camps or fleeing from place to place as helpless refugees. Appreciating their courage and bravery, she bereaves their destiny:

> "They used to be so full of life, these friends of mine, so unafraid of the future which they thought they were going to mould into a brave new world of peace and plenty. But it was not to be. Their dreams were rudely shattered and who knows if they will ever be recaptured." (Hutheesing 48)

With exuberance and enthusiasm, Krishna Hutheesing describes her journey to Europe. Here we find Krishna full of hope, confidence and aspiration. Krishna gets first-hand knowledge of European culture and civilisation during this tour. In this tour of Europe, we meet a spirited Krishna full of vigor and power, playing adventure games like mountaineering and trekking with Jawaharlal and other Swiss and American friends. Wherever she went, she made many friends, of all nationalities, mostly students and artists. Krishna actively participated in the adventure activities like climbing which shows her grit and her love for sports and adventure activities. Along with her brother Jawahar and other friends of his, Krishna joined the excursions tours organised during weekends of the school. She learned ski and skate as well while in Europe.

Recalling this journey, she writes that the happiest time she spent was in Switzerland and Paris. In later life, Krishna often wished to go back to those days when life was carefree and joyous and wanted to meet old friends again. Though plans were made repeatedly, they never materialized. Her father later joined her on this tour, and along with other family members, she went to Russia. Her father and brother were invited to attend the tenth Anniversary celebrations of Russian Revolution. She attended a huge state banquet given in honor of all the guests of the Soviet Government. In the banquet where the meal was a lengthy affair, unknowingly she gulped vodka as she thought it was water, her throat burned, and her eyes smarted with tears (55). Her Russian visit had been brief, but it was a vital experience. What struck her most were the determination and the new spirit of hope that moved everyone she met. She fervently hoped that these Russian would one day succeed in creating a happier society, which would better the state of humanity all over the world.

Wellness expert Noma Nazish suggests that "Facing difficulties in an unfamiliar environment, among new people, forces you to learn and adapt to a life out of your comfort zone. This makes you more flexible, patient and emotionally strong (Nazish)". When Krishna leaves for Ahmedabad for the first time after her marriage, her husband Raja compares her shifting to the new city to the uprooting of a young tree. He felt as if he were uprooting a young tree that had been planted in a certain soil where it had grown and blossomed. Now it was to be replanted elsewhere and many doubts assailed him. He had doubts in his mind whether the tree would be benefited by this uprooting and become more beautiful and fruitful, or would it wither away in strange surroundings. This migration from central India to western India had a deep impact on Krishna's cultural identity as she was now with a business class vegetarian Gujarati family. Krishna adapts to new ways of living and thinking after her marriage.

In her book *Narratology: Introduction to the Theory of Narrative* Mieke Bal writes that in many travel stories, the movement is a goal in itself.

It is expected to result in a change, liberation, introspection, wisdom, or knowledge (Bal 140). When we go through this breathtakingly fascinating autobiography, we find Krishna Hutheesing undertaking sojourns to unknown places and discern each travel experience having a long lasting impact on her psychological and emotional growth.

References

Bal, Mieke. *Narratology: Introduction to the Theory of Narrative.* 3rd Ed. Toronto: TUP, 2009.

Hoffman, Edward. "How Travels Spurs Personal Growth". 13 Feb. 2020. Web. 26 Aug 2021. "https://www.psychologytoday.com/us/blog/the-peak-experience/202002/how-travels-spurs personal-growth"

Hutheesing, Krishna Nehru. *With No Regrets: An Autobiography*. New York: The John Day Company, 1945.

Jain, Jasbir. "The Difficulty of Writing/Reading the Self." *Literary Constructs of the Self: Socio-Cultural Contexts.* Ed. Santosh Gupta and Mini Nanda. Jaipur: Rawat Pub., 2010. 63-80.

Kashdan, Todd B. "The Mental Benefits of Vacationing Somewhere New". *Harvard Business Review.* 26 January 2018. Web. 21 Aug 2021. "https://hbr.org/2018/01/the-mental-benefits-of-vacationing-somewhere-new"

Nazish, Noma. "Five Reasons Why Travel Is Good For Your Mental Health" Forbs. 22 Jan. 2018. Web. 30 Aug. 2021. "https://www.forbes.com/sites/nomanazish/2018/01/22/five-reasons-why-travel-is-good-for-your-mental-health/?sh=31f4eab55934"

Soja, Edward W. *Postmodern Geographies: The Reassertion of Space in Critical Social Theory.* London: Verso, 1989.

CHAPTER 3

Travelling: Aspects, Concepts and Philosophy

Ambika Gahlot and Anant Pandey

Abstract

In this modern day and age where even fictional concepts like multiverses could turn into reality, it is only plausible to assume that everything has different dimensions. It depends on how we perceive things and how we shape our outlook towards them. The concept of 'traveling' isn't something that is a by-product of living in a civilised society. The traces of humans travelling for miles can be dated back to the primitive ages when even the concept of means of transport was alien to us. As a species we used to cover immeasurable distances on bare foot for the sake of survival but as humans advanced forward, it soon started taking shape of a recreational activity.

In this research paper, we have taken a look at different dimensions and aspects of traveling by taking examples from our daily lives into consideration. Traveling as a concept makes you drown in it, while you wonder what lies ahead. Be it discovering your own self, to help someone in need, to break the shackles of monotony or to go in search of the self, we all have our own reasons to travel and this research paper majorly focuses on why people travel. This article aims to throw some light on the various aspects related to travelling. A human is a social animal and thus, loves to be in company of others. His travel is induced by many reasons such as passion, glory, for professional reasons – job or business, migration for work, pilgrimage, to break the monotonous cycle, and when he has existential crises. The article is an attempt to underline the key aspects of traveling.

'People travel to wonder,
At the height of the mountains,
At the huge waves of the seas,
At the long course of the rivers,
At the vast compass of the ocean,
At the circular motion of the stars,
And yet they pass by themselves without wondering.'

St Augustine

Keywords: Travel, monotony, passion, glory, soul searching, political reasons, migration, business, trade, rejuvenation.

"There is a pleasure in the pathless woods,
There is rupture on the lonely shore,
There is society where none intrudes,
By the deep sea and the music in its roar,
I love not man the less but nature more."

ord Byron

Traveling is a phenomenon. A process that begins the day, a mother conceives a baby in the womb, a journey that gives us all sorts of experiences. Someone has rightly said 'Life is a bumpy ride'. It is never the same. We never learn this much from the books that way we learn from being to new places, meeting with different kinds of people, experiencing varied cultures and eating a variety of cuisines. Education comes not just intact in the books but experiencing life as it comes to us. Our reaction to the situations, our actions, and our equilibrium tell a lot of our survival instincts. Our soul yearns for such kinds of adventures and situations that make us feel alive. The popular television show 'Man versus Wild' is one such example. It showcases how our instincts improve being into the extreme situations and how man has this innate talent to survive without using any technical equipment just by learning a few basic survival tricks and having a knowledge of nature.

Traveling imparts us skills that can never be inculcated just by formal education. Alfred Lord Tennyson's 'Ulysses' comes to mind, when Tennyson says, "How dull it is to pause, to make an end, To rust unburnished, not to shine in use!"" Traveling gives a new experience of life, whereas, monotony tends to make us weak, bodily and mentally. Travelling sharpens our instincts. It gives us a chance to understand things in a better life and to look at life from all possible angles. We meet ourselves in different lights. James Joyce's Ulysses has some insights to offer too. He says, "Every life is in many days, day after day. We walk through ourselves, meeting robbers, ghosts, giants, old men, young men, wives, widows, brothers-in-love, but always meeting ourselves." How traveling is in a way a sort of unravelling the latent. How it is a process of metamorphosis. It never touches you physically yet changes the course of your thinking and impacts your thought process vibrantly. It gives us this unique opportunity to experience our own existence and be touched by the existence of others. To have our own stories and experiences to share and to be enriched by those who have travelled before.

Father of empiricism Francis Bacon in his essay "Of Travels" enlists the benefit of traveling and demarks the things to keep in mind before traveling.

The various reasons for which one take the road, are as follows:

> Every year thousands of people travel to pay homage to their deities, meet adoration to Gods, seek blessings and start life afresh.
>
> 'Life is a pilgrimage. The wise man does not rest by the roadside inns. He marches direct to the illimitable domain of eternal bliss, his ultimate destination'.
>
> Sivananda

The literal definition of Pilgrimage is 'a long journey that a person makes to visit a religious place' but when we look at the real life examples laid bare in front of us, it is safe to assume that it is so much more than that. Every year, countless devotees find themselves embarking on an adventure-filled spiritual journey, taking them to their respective religions most sacred and holy places. It is sort of uncanny that despite having different mind-sets, perspectives and their own set of problems, every pilgrim is bound by one single thing – spirituality.

People who embark upon such voyages don't take it just as a 'task' that needs to be fulfilled in order to attain divinity. It is the journey that matters more. Rigorous paths, unpredictable weather coupled with scenic views splattered all over the landscape combine together to deliver an enthralling experience. Some seek redemption while some just want to seek divinity in their respective quests. The maligned minds of humans slowly make way for piousness similar to an infant's consciousness, as you inch closer to the gongs reverberating from the temples or the chants echoing from a mosque for that matter. When you find yourself troubled with the worldly affairs, you seek assistance from an external force that drives this whole universe and that is when one should take up such a journey that will not only lead you to a sacred destination but will also rinse your soul in the process.

Thousands of devotees every year march towards the Ramdev Baba Temple in Rajasthan, situated at Ramdevra, 13 km from Pokhran in Jaisalmer district. During the month of August-September, all the connecting highways that lead to Ramdevra are filled with devotees traveling for hundreds of kilometres, either barefoot or on their commuter motorcycles. As an experienced motorcyclist, I can testify that travelling hundreds of kilometres on a commuter motorcycle without any proper riding equipment is not an easy feat. Not only has this, a major chunk of devotees also taken up this herculean task on their foot, mothers carrying their infants on their back while the patriarch of the family drags along the luggage is a sight to behold. In the wake of completing the journey, they have to battle the scorching heat waves of the arid lands of Rajasthan that could even put the infamous wild west of the USA to shame.

India isn't devoid of such pilgrimages. In fact, you would find such spiritual voyages in every nook and cranny of this vast, vibrant country. Pilgrimages that lead straight into the lap of the mighty Himalayas also deserve a special mention here. The Himalayas might be filled with natural grandeur but it has its own set of risks and uncertainties. Frequent landslides, bone-chilling breezes and other related factors make sure that traveling in the mountains isn't easy. And yet, to answer the call of the almighty, thousands of devotees flock towards the mountains for treacherous treks like Kedarnath, Amarnath, Kailash Mansarovar and the likes. The journey might not be, but the goal is rather simple – to experience divinity in its most pious and grand form.

There's something magnetic that drives you towards such journeys. The fast-paced nature of this competitive world has successfully managed to drift us away from our spirituality and what better way to fill ourselves again with eternal bliss than to embark on an adventure-filled journey to God's own abode? This would be the prime reason why I would try to embark on the Tungnath Trek, otherwise known as the world's highest temple dedicated to Lord Shiva. The goal would be simple – to spend a few days in the lap of Himalayas, trying to take all the grandeur in and tread towards the peak to chant 'Mahamrityunjay' mantra as the heavenly spirit watches upon me.

Another interesting reason which induces travelling is to break the monotony.

> 'Every man can transform the world from one of monotony and drabness to one of excitement and adventure.
>
> Irving Wallace

The modern-era has brought with it the age of hustling where one cannot score big in life without grinding tirelessly for hours on a regular basis. Hustling, the word itself might sound cool because of baseless motivational quotes floating on all the social media handles but like every possible thing in this universe, it has its flip side too and it is not pretty as one might imagine. With Hustling, monotony comes complimentary. These notorious twins can damage one's mindset to such an extent that it could drain the life out of someone. Monotony doesn't kill you with a swift blow like a lightning strike, it is more of a cloudy, gloomy day that grows on you, slowly sucking the endorphins out of your system.

Almost everyone we come across in our professional and personal lives are bound in the shackles of Monotony. We wake up at the same time, follow the same regime every day, take the same route to our respective workplaces and moreover, we interact with the same set of individuals. Sure, human beings are social animals and our rather mundane life does help to fill our pockets with the much-needed moolah to survive but on the other hand, we also crave for new experiences. The realisation of becoming just a breathing yet lifeless creature hits hard and that is exactly when traveling arrives, riding on a white horse, draped in armor gilded from fine Lannister gold… just to save you from getting drowned in the black sea called monotony.

And when this happens, it is best to take the helping hand rather than struggling to breathe when monotony fills up your precious lungs. The dreariness of a mundane lifestyle can easily be cured if you set out on the wide open road, cutting all your ties with your tedious life for a while. It isn't an absolute necessity to find an exotic location and break your bank just to get there. We live in a beautiful country which is abundant with lush-green forests, mystical mountains, riveting rivers and golden deserts. What's more important is to just set yourself free and get out there. Once you have taken the leap, let everything unfold in its own natural manner. Go where the roads are taking you, open your helmet's lid or roll down the windows of your car to take in all the aroma this nature has to offer. Rather sitting on a cliff and pondering about 'what could have been' of your life, stare at the gorgeous views our mother nature has bestowed this planet with. These experiences are bound to act as an ailment to your disease called monotony. It is essential to experience something 'mighty and mystical' in your life like snow-capped mountain peaks becoming one with the clouds, just to comprehend that your own problems and lifestyle are miniscule in this grand scheme of things.

Take the 2013 movie 'The Secret Life of Walter Mitty' for instance, in which the protagonist Walter Mitty leads the exact same lifestyle as discussed above and often finds himself zoned out on multiple occasions. When he's zoned out, he often finds himself in adventurous situations that are basically non-existent in his actual life. Shortly after, he goes on an action-packed, romantic voyage. After this visual masterpiece comes to an end, you would want to buy a rucksack, grab your rosary and go out on an adventure to explore the world, melting all the shackles you have been chained with.

Survival is one major aspect that cannot be avoided while considering the various aspects of traveling.

> 'I was amazed that what I needed to survive could be carried on my back. And, most surprising of all, that I could carry it.'
>
> Cheryl Strayed

One of the many things that make animals different from plants is survival instincts. A plant cannot dodge a blow from an axe but an animal can do whatever it takes just to survive and sway away from potential danger. Humans are no different in this regard. We take drastic measures just to ensure that we survive. And sometimes it involves travelling miles and miles, just to make sure that your lineage lives to tell the story. There are different aspects that can force a human to undertake a long voyage for survival. Be it harsh climate, religious conflicts, natural calamities or a pandemic outbreak.

The Exodus of Kashmiri Hindus or the Exodus of Kashmiri Pandits can be seen as a prime example of traveling countless miles just for the sake of survival due to a religious conflict. After Independence-seeking militant groups provoked a Muslim-dominated insurgency in the state of Jammu and Kashmir in 1989, anti-Hindu attacks and pogroms became a regular affair. Approximately 3 lakhs to 6 lakh Kashmiri Pandits used to reside in J&K in 1990 and in 2016, only 2,000-3,000 remain in their native state. While some of them managed to flee and relocate in different parts of our country, those who couldn't, were killed.

Another major reason why humans are forced to migrate from one place to another is harsh climate. The Himalayas might be the mightiest mountain ranges in the whole wide world with breathtaking sceneries splattered all across the landscape but they can also turn monstrous in a matter of days. Strong blizzards, heavy snowfall and temperatures dropping even below than the hell down under make the terrain absolutely inhabitable in the winter season. I recall from my personal experience while riding through the Ladakh region that some farmers that call the Pangong Tso Lake their abode, have to migrate towards Leh city when the winter comes. Travelling in the mountains sounds adventurous to us but for them, it becomes a matter of survival.

The past one year has also showcased countless examples of people migrating for their dear life. As the pandemic struck our country with a mighty force, the authorities had to enforce a nationwide lockdown. Thousands of people lost their jobs and their way of earning. The people, who previously migrated towards metro cities, seeking employment or a source of income, had to migrate back towards their native places. Trains were flocked with people and most of them also had to cover their journey back home barefoot. With no public transport at their dispense, some of these helpless migrants also lost their lives while undertaking this treacherous journey.

This is another dimension of travelling that doesn't come to light that often. Travelling isn't just about quenching your wanderlust or to generate some content for your social media. Just like the moon, it has its dark side too. Just like Charles Darwin said, "It is not the strongest of the species that survive, nor the most intelligent, but the one most responsive to change". And sometimes the best response can be-pack your belongings and take the road!

Travelling is all the more crucial when we look at the local workers travelling every day for the sake of survival. Workers cross borders every day to earn their daily wages and this migration becomes crucial for economy as well. It's not about the destination but the glory of the ride!

Most of the people that we come across every day, have created a fine boundary around their life. They fear crossing that line in order to get classified by the society as sane and sensible. The doctrine of 'how to become a basic human' reads that a human only needs basic things to feel content in their life: a professional career, an abode to share your life with your companion and a couple of children whom you can pass on the same 'basics' of human life. But there's a special breed of adventurous souls whom you cannot bind inside those boundaries. They cross those limits to become limitless. While most of us seek completion in some or the other way, they seek glory.

To achieve glory, a human can tread down different paths. Some might make use of their mental horses, their intellect to shape the way we look at this physical world but the adventurous souls that we are talking about here, take a different path altogether, a rugged, treacherous and bumpy path. They transform into inter-continental ballistic missiles to achieve glory, munching miles after miles on their trusted machines. These glory-seekers are not to be confused with globetrotters because they don't travel to seek themselves, to explore or to seek the meaning of life. They travel to break previous records, win an acclaimed tournament and to show the world what a human can achieve!

Take the Dakar Rally for instance. Touted as the World's Toughest Rally, it invites rally riders and drivers from across the globe to complete a circuit of around 8,000-9,000 kilometres over a span of 10-15 days. Although the whole rally is divided into multiple stages, the participants have to cover hundreds of kilometres every day. It is an endurance race that tests the limits of a human that how long one can keep it together. What makes it the toughest and most dangerous rally in the world is the terrain. The rallyists have to navigate through oceans of sand and rugged train. No tarmac or cemented road whatsoever, it is just you, your machine and the wilderness. Even finishing the rally in one piece is considered a huge achievement.

If this isn't insane enough, there's also an even tougher category dubbed 'Malle Moto'. Generally, the participants have a support team with them that helps them with the maintenance of their motorcycles when a stage ends but in Malle Moto, you are on your own, in a literal fashion. You are allowed to carry a crate with you that consists all the spare parts and the basic things you might require in the rally. The rider or the driver who registers in this category, has to work on its trusted machine himself, without any assistance. After battling the tough terrain at mind-numbing speeds accompanied with heat waves, they have to service their machines and plan the route for the next day as the cold breeze of the desert freeze their bones in the night.

Being such a long, daring and dangerous event, the Dakar is also unfortunately shrouded in great tragedy. Since 1979, 76 people are known to have died as a result of the Dakar rally. But that doesn't stop this special breed from participating and circumnavigating the vast deserts because they seek glory. Some people might not consider this as traveling but they are covering a mammoth distance, coming across spectacular sceneries, becoming one with the terrain and battling things unimaginable to a 'basic' human mind. This is exactly what makes this sort of travel absolutely glorious!

'Soul searching', the term often has been overused in many of the blogs, articles and social media platforms. The whole definition of 'Soul searching' is to find oneself. In the humdrum of this century we have left the peace behind. Peace which keeps us going. It keeps us sane. Often we find ourselves torn, irritated and bewildered in the traumatic experiences life throws at us. Often we seek redemption for the sins we have committed, knowingly or unknowingly. We feel the world goes on and on. No matter if our pace gets obstructed. Reasons are many, the loss of a near and dear one, job pressure, responsibility which makes us stoop, or any other consideration. We feel we are trapped. Trapped in the everyday chores we merely exist. Life needs a break. Break not to quit and never come again, but break to rejuvenate and come back again with double the intensity and zeal. Robert Frost the famous American Poet has beautifully concluded his poem "Birches" by the lines

> "I'd like to get away from earth awhile
> And then come back to it and begin over.
> May no fate wilfully misunderstand me
> And half grant what I wish and snatch me away
> Not to return. Earth's the right place for love:"

How beautifully the poet delineates the concept of taking a break and rejuvenating. Soul searching is a similar process. Humans are trapped in the process of life. This life is not meant for fulfilling materialistic pursuits. Life has a deep meaning. Our aspirations and desires sometimes become the root of heartaches. We feel trapped in the materialistic world. Travel at that time may prove to be of greater purpose. When we visit places, see the mendicants, the troubles faced by people, the slums, the pathetic conditions people are living in we realise how artificial our lives have become. We run after money and popularity. Fame is nothing but a lure. Travel is all the more important for search who we are. What is the greatest purpose of life, why God made humans different from all other life forms? There are several mediation camps that offer a soul searching experience for people to make them feel the purity of their soul and calm them. These can be found in Himalayan regions, Nepal borders and other serene places. The mediation camps are distributed all over the globe like Ireland, Thailand, Alaska, South Africa etc. Apart from mediation these camps have a lot to offer. They teach yoga, how to live a balanced life, and how to cut toxicity out of life. Nature has a lot to offer only if we are willing to take.

The founder of Buddhism, Gautama Buddha comes to mind when we dive into the concept of travel for soul searching. Born into an aristocratic family, Lord Buddha left home at the age of 29 in search for the meaning of life. In his quest, he travelled to a great many places, until finally attaining enlightenment in Bodh Gaya India, under the Mahabodhi Tree that still stands today in Bihar, India. His sermons have travelled a lot and his followers are spread all across the world. Buddhism is a religion that imparts peace and calls for the need of Soul searching.

Existential crises or Existential anxiety is also a reason for people to undertake journey. Existential crisis may occur when a person frequently wonders whether or not life has any inherent meaning or purpose. A person may also question their own existence within a world that might seem meaningless. When the pressure is real and we don't find any answers, it is better to pack our bags and travel. Travel is soothing. Experiences change our outlook about life. We find peace within. This is also a reason to know oneself is important. People often lose track, life seem haphazard and things don't work out. We question our existence. In search of answers we travel. We explore, in the process we mature and gradually learn to calm down. Travel is one such phenomenon in this regard. It brings us back to life.

> "Do not be satisfied by the stories that come before you. Unfold your own myth."
>
> – Rumi.

Soul searching is one such aspect in the movies of Imtiaz Ali. The famous Indian film director has made movies keeping in mind the aspect of Soul searching and traveling. Movies like Rockstar, Jab we met, Tamasha, Highway have a beautiful traveling background as a part of narration.

"Tamasha" is about the journey of someone who has lost his edge in trying to follow acceptable conventions of society. The film is based on the central theme of abrasion and loss of self that happens in an attempt to find oneself. How society makes us a puppet. How the individual is shattered under the pressure of aligning with the social norms. All stories are same and yet one needs to find their own story. A film that almost mocks us by showcasing the monotonous life we have succumbed to. It is literally shouting at us. Asking us to separate from the herd we have comfortably blended into. It decodes every single string in a person's heart, ponders over the problem of becoming a soul-less robot & pushes the boundaries of existentialism in a glimmering, colourful stage of life. The central character wants to become a story teller but isn't allowed to do what he enjoys the most. Thus, loses the gusto for his plans to travel to Corsica for the much needed break. He needs to search the long lost answers. What is he doing, why is he doing and the implications to follow. The travel proves to be a turning point in his life and he decides to give his forgotten passion another shot. It dawns on him. He seeks to find happiness and the travel makes it worth it.

"Highway" is another cinematic masterpiece of Imtiaz Ali. It showcases a kidnap and how travel works as a therapy at times. The therapeutic effects of traveling are showcased in the movie. It involves abduction, but in order to hide the girl the kidnapper keeps on travelling and in the process they experience life with vivacity. The experiences teach them to grow with nature and travel is thus a crucial element of the narrative.

Imtiaz Ali's Highway is about escape. It is a dreamlike film, complete with achingly beautiful Himalayan landscapes and vast, unpopulated, dusty expanses. The movie shows the process of meeting with oneself and the feeling of liberation. Journey is so much better than the destination and the movie validate it on so many levels.

Another masterpiece which comes to mind is the Hollywood movie "Into the wild". It is an American biographical adventure drama film director by Sean Penn. The movie is an adaptation of the 1996 non-fiction book of the same name written by Jon Krakauer and tells the story of Christopher McCandless ("Alexander Supertramp"), a man who hiked across North America into the Alaskan wilderness in the early 1990s. The movie is based on a true story. This is a reflective, regretful, serious film about a young man swept away by his uncompromising choices. He keeps journals in which he sees himself in the third person as a heroic loner, renouncing civilisation, returning to the embrace of nature. In centuries past such men might have been saints, retreating to a cave or hidden hermitage, denying themselves all pleasures except subsistence. He sees himself not as homeless, but as a man freed from homes. He tells how his strange experiences shape his consciousness and he starts to live into the wild. What he mostly saw was the glory of the North American landscape west of the Mississippi: the ancient woodlands of the Pacific Northwest, the canyons and deserts farther south, the wheat fields of the northern prairie and Alaska, a place that Mr. McCandless seemed to regard with almost mystical reverence. Chris is in many ways the intellectual heir of 19th-century writer-naturalists like John Muir and especially Henry David Thoreau, whose uncompromising idealism – "rather than love, than money, than fame, give me truth" – he takes as a watchword. His credo is perhaps most succinctly stated by Thoreau's mentor Ralph Waldo Emerson, who advised that "the ancient precept, 'Know thyself,' and the modern precept, 'Study Nature,' become at last one maxim." He gets to know what is soul was yearning for and settles in Alaska leaving every materialistic aspect of life behind.

Such cinematic masterpieces advocate the soul searching principle of travelling.

Traveling has professional aspects as well. People of our likes, travelled extensively to draft out the world as we know it today, from the tiny islands of the Oceania, to the countries as big as America, and had to be travelled to be known. From the languages to the literature, rulers to religions, clothes to cuisines, it all travelled either to sell or to be sold. Man first travelled to explore, to know the unknown lands, to know the new races, landscapes, resources etc, and then to rule those lands and races and sell the resources. Travel cannot be separated from the history of the world economics. Humans have been travelling since centuries for work, for education, for research, for exploration and trade and for excursions.

All the major empires globally started from their travel for trade. Centuries later, we still travel for work, more efficiently than ever via skies, land and seas. Whether to attend a self-developing conference in Singapore or to get that master's degree from Germany we continue to travel. In the modern times, with the changing dynamics there are various reasons people travel for work. We see people migrating on student visas to various countries and end up living the rest of their lives there and we also see people going to the UAE in the morning to attend meeting and flying back home to have dinner with their kids. The world as it is called today is a global village and with humans progressing at exceptional rate, this village is more connected than ever. It just takes us hours to cover thousands of kilometres. Amid the covid-19 pandemic countries of Europe, Middle East and Africa, this trend of movement is more of a lifestyle. A trader would buy goods from the country A to sell it in the country B. A student would sign up for a university over the borders. Some move around to cover a news story or some just move because they love to. An English man would move down to South Korea to teach them his language and to learn their lifestyle. Rulers used to move slaves for the labour needs and in a much better world today, we chose to move ourselves to fulfil the labour needs abroad. Outsourcing has induced travel and people are lured by better remuneration to change their native country in a hope of better life.

To travel is to ameliorate; everything is like add on to one's personality. The pizza travelled from Italy to our tables and the coffee travelled from Ethiopia to bless our mornings. The tea too travels far across the world to help people have a fresh and exotic morning experience. Today people order bright flowers, seasonal food and many more peculiar stuff from all across the globe and traveling thus becomes a universal phenomenon not just for humans but it does good to non-living things as well.

From saving few cents to be making dollars, people and products keep on travelling. That new cell phone you are saving for, was designed in the office complexes of California and made in industries of China. It was moved to China to save those cents and would be moved to you to make those dollars. Our oceans sail tones of everything at all times. Our ancestors made the silk routes, the sea ports and we continue to build the road networks and the cargo airplanes just with the goals of being more efficient every day, to make the travel seamless. We have evolved to make travel more beneficial not just for our mental health and peace but also to procure monetary benefits. Special and dedicated trade routes are made to transform commodities and cargo. Be it the Suez Canal, Panama Canal or the Silk route. We never know how much the food on our table has travelled before being served on the table. If we give it a thought it is fascinating.

With the advances today, we have made ourselves capable of moving aids to flooded villages and soldiers to the battlefields. With our will to move, we will continue to travel; maybe to learn a new skill, to feed our families or just for the sake of movement. We learnt to explore from the birds flying in the free skies, moving over the deep oceans and the dense forests. Travel is something we have been doing from the most ancient times. Be it for the search of food or the search of spices, the exploration of new lands, the discovery has always proved fruitful for human race. Traveling has become integral for civilisation. We continue to enhance our skills even today by traveling to different parts of the world and imbibing in us the peculiar traits of those regions.

Today the concept of traveling is not just limited to the planet Earth but people are also exploring with more dynamic concepts. Space travel is one such example. The billionaire Jeff Bezos has turned this concept into a reality on 20th July, 2021. Bezos has made a short journey to space, in the first crewed flight of his rocket ship, New Shepard. He was accompanied by Mark Bezos, his brother, Wally Funk, an 82-year-old pioneer of the space race, and an 18-year-old student. They travelled in a capsule with the biggest windows flown in space, offering stunning views of the Earth. When the capsule touched back down after the 10-minute, 10-second flight, Jeff Bezos exclaimed: "Best day ever!" Travel makes us feel, we experience our existence and that is rare. It makes us feel alive. Travel does us good.

Traveling has induced a lot of economic prosperity as well. Tourism provides jobs where they are needed the most – and most of the time, tourism is a driver of job growth and a healthy economy. Tourism is a major contributor to the economy. Bahamas, Maldives, Andaman and Nicobar Islands, St. Lucia, Dominica, Jamaica, Cambodia, Georgia, etc. attract tourists all over the year. A major part of their economy is based on travel and tourism. New forms of economic activities have developed over time. Hotels, resorts, Airbnb concepts are developing. New ventures and start-ups are erupting. New professions are emerging. Travel has induced a lot of economic prosperity. A lot of economic activities are dependent directly or indirectly on travel and tourism. Small scale businesses, local artisans and workers are now getting positioned on the world map because of travel and tourism. People now save a part of their salary just to travel and explore the diverse, unpopular, sparsely populated places which were previously hidden from the world. The youth have started ventures to encourage people to travel and create awareness about the environment more. Increasing number of blogs, videos and reels are a proof that the world is becoming conscious of its horizons and people love to cater to the needs of nature as well.

Some people possess insane love for traveling. They nurture this passion to a level that they make records and break records every day. So passion is the next vital aspect in line that cannot be ignored.

> "Twenty years from now you will be more disappointed by the things that you didn't do than by the ones that you did do. So throw off the bowlines and sail away from the safe harbour. Catch the trade winds in your sails. Explore. Dream, Discover."
>
> Mark Twain

Each one of us is driven by something. That could be your ambition, goals but what makes us truly alive and not just a breathing specimen of flesh and bones is passion. Passion is like that fire that keeps you warm on the coldest of nights. It is that silver lining that gets formed around the dark clouds. Every individual out there has its own passion but what sets apart passionate travellers is their hunger for meeting new people, treading down unexplored terrains and coming across breath taking landscapes.

Emilio Scotto is one such adventurer who hails from Argentina and holds the world record for the longest ever journey by a motorcycle. Over the span of around 10 years, he covered around 485,000 miles on his two-wheeled steed and ticked off 232 countries and territories from his list. During his long-legged journey, he circumnavigated the entire world and not just once but twice! He got imprisoned 6 times, robbed 5 times and collided 9 times. While circumnavigating the entire planet, he got to witness one major earthquake, two tornadoes and four hurricanes. During his journey, he clicked 90,000 photographs.

Travel is a form of liberation. Walt Whitman's "The Song of the open road" is one such poem which lays bare before us the various aspects of travel and freedom. The poem connects the process of traveling on the open road with the liberation and salvation soul. Originally published as "Poem of the Road", the poem is divided in fifteen sections.

Essentially a dramatic monologue, the poem is divisible into three "movements": the persona's absorption of the road's sights and sounds and his translation of them into a visionary consciousness, his Trans figurative voice conjuring up visions of limitless possibilities, and his quasi-oratorical call to companions to undertake the mystic trek. In the first "movement" – with its exuberant apostrophe to the mystic road – his perception and his inner sight merge: the road and everything on it become a nexus of symbols. He reads these symbols inscribed on the road's ostensibly "impassive" surfaces and interprets them for everyone's benefit. The experience fills him with a sense of transcendence. Envisioning a race of perfect men and women, he exclaims: "I think I could stop here myself and do miracles.. . . I ordain myself loosed of limits and imaginary lines. . . my own master total and absolute". Although the poem is esteemed for its evocation of nature and wanderlust, it contains little description of nature. Rather, nature becomes an extension of the persona's capacious imagination, for, as Whitman elsewhere explains, nature is always filtered through the mind of the observer. The poet celebrates the out of doors and the road in particular, as a space where men can come together in a meaningful way, where status and social markers matter less. It celebrates a communion and a democracy based on place.

"Allons! Whoever you are come travel with me!
Traveling with me you find what never tires."

The poet invites all alike to come with him and journey along the open road. This life is a journey leading to the eternal which is the destination.

"Allons! We must not stop here,
However sweet these laid-up stores, however convenient this dwelling we cannot remain here"

In the above lines, emphasis is placed on going, on moving, on arising and on travelling. The poet describes what happiness feels like. The essence of existence is to move forward and experience life as it comes. He says:

"The efflux of the soul is happiness, here is happiness,
I think it pervades the open air, waiting at all times,
Now it flows unto us, we are rightly charged."

Whitman has used layers of meaning in the poem but primarily the poem deals with his carefree spirit and robust optimism. An attitude that best comes out when you travel on the open road. He concludes the poem with a message, extending his hand with a personal invitation to explore life, to be a wanderer, to travel and liberate oneself.

"Camerado, I give you my hand!
I give you my love more precious than money,

I give you myself before preaching or law;
Will you give me yourself? Will you come travel with me?
Shall we stick by each other as long as we live?"

Travel ameliorates life, it shapes our consciousness and fills our life with memories. It drives people to achieve unachievable feats, opens our eyes to new experiences and teaches things no school or college ever could! So pack your bags and get out there!

References

Jasbir Jain, "Strings of Gold An Anthology of Poems Part 3", "Ulysses By Alfred Lord Tennyson" Whitman, Walt. "Song of the open Road" 1856

Frost, Robert. "Mountain Interval" "Birches", 1916

Byron, Lord. "Childe Harold's Pilgrimage", "There is pleasure in the pathless woods",

https://poets.org/poem/childe-harolds-pilgrimage-there-pleasure-pathless-woods

Times of India, Jeff Bezos Space Travel, https://timesofindia.indiatimes.com /world/us/how-blue-origins-jeff-bezos-will-soar-into-space/articleshow/ 84522491.cms, 20 July, 2021

https://en.wikipedia.org/wiki/Gautama_Buddha

CHAPTER 4

The Cambridge Chronicles

Dr. Urvashi Sabu

Abstract

In Autumn 2018, I was awarded the Charles Wallace India Trust Translation Fellowship to the British Centre for Literary Translation (BCLT), University of East Anglia, Norwich UK. Those ten weeks, from October to December, turned out to be an exploration and investigation of all the identities I thought I had acquired in my two score and some years. My definitions of myself and of the 'Other' were turned upside down. I lived a life I had imagined only in my dreams. For that brief flicker of time, I became the woman I had always wanted to be: intrepid traveler, wide eyed explorer, curious student, and ardent learner. I had the good fortune of meeting and knowing some very interesting and wonderful people, and of creating lasting bonds from chance encounters. This visit to the UK became a parenthesis in the sentence of my life, everything that had transpired before faded into insignificance as I navigated this experience, fully, to the brim, to the last drop; until my senses were surfeit and my past, just a memory. Needless to say, coming back to India, to 'home' and 'family', took on unanticipated connotations.

Presented in the pages below is a vignette of one such day from my yet unpublished daily journal of this stint: a day visit to the University town of Cambridge with Duncan Large, the Academic Director of the BCLT, UEA, Norwich UK.

Keywords: Identity, Exploration, Experience, life, Home.

9th November, 2018

Cambridge with Duncan, by Duncan today! But first, I have to wake up at 7:00 am. to reach university by 10:00, in order to attend a one hour workshop on 'Translating Philosophy'. Duncan is taking this workshop with first year students of PPL (Politics, Philosophy, and Language). The venue for this workshop is a room in the minus two basement of the Zuckerman Institute on campus. It's a terribly hush-hush place where you cannot open a single door without tapping your campus card across a dangerous looking red light. And so we find ourselves, Duncan and I, in a space called the Virtual Reality Room, with dark walls and surreal equipment that looks like a scene from Star Trek, but is likely cameras, projectors, pipes, and tripods. Why on earth this room would be allotted to a PPL class, for God's sake! I wonder as I take in the unlikely surroundings where we are about to launch a discussion on philosophy and translation. Anyway, we're soon face to face with a motley crowd of seven students who've managed to extricate themselves from the warm comfort of their beds on a *Friday* morning to attend this workshop; and going by their hair, their clothes and the absolutely somnambulant expression on their faces, that's just about all that they've managed to do. Duncan has brought along, for this workshop, five translations of a passage from Plato's *Symposium*; starting with PB Shelley's in 1818 to the latest by Albert Anderson in 2003. It's a slightly racy passage on the nature of love. As he distributes the handouts to the students, he explains what must be done. He divides them into two groups and asks them to get going. The students begin the task of reading the translations, and discussing which is better, which not as good, and why. But after 20 minutes of giggling amidst their internal discussions, one student with decisively green hair hits the nail on the head when she says, 'So according to this passage, every person has to be either adulterous or gay?' If it wasn't for the fact that I was in a class, I'd have fallen off my chair in disbelieving laughter. But this *is* a class, and Duncan, after giving a patient and smiling hearing to green-hair, sets about analysing the translations with them. The hour is soon over, the workshop done, the students stream out of the Star Trek set, and we make our way to the parking lot to set out for the trip.

Duncan spends some time meandering between the rows of vehicles, trying to locate his car. I'm quite intrigued that he doesn't remember where he parked it just a couple of hours earlier; and when I voice this in the form of a question, he answers in the negative, adding that it's a new BMW he's only bought 'last week'. Could that be a coincidence? I wonder, as I recall how just a few days ago my new friend Helen and I traveled across Kent, Dover and Canterbury in her BMW convertible, which she too had only just bought 'last week'. Duncan sums it up quite effectively, 'Well, it seems people are laying out their BMWs for you!' And we're off on this pleasant sunny day, to his home town Cambridge. Throughout the hour long drive, Duncan fills me up on direction coordinates, the countryside, and the road and rail system between Norwich and Cambridge, in true professional tour guide style. Soon, we hit the town, and as we cruise along tree lined, shady, and broad roads bordered by neat, well-kept cottages and university buildings, he points to the street on which he lives. We're not stopping there however, because we're scheduled to meet his partner Sheila for lunch at Newnham College, where she is a faculty member.

We breeze in through the electronic security at Newnham since Duncan, with faculty spouse privileges, has the code. Then, we're knocking at a door that has 'Dr Sheila Watts' displayed on a nameplate, and a cheery 'come in!' greets us from within. We open the door and step in. Nothing has prepared me for the Sheila I see rising from her desk and briskly moving forward to meet us. Somehow, I had imagined a trim brunette with coiffed hair, in a fitted dress and high heels, with just the right amount of uppityness a Newnham faculty would possess. Instead, I see a much older (than Duncan), pleasing, straw haired maternal figure in a jumper and pants walk up to us with a broad smile and arms outstretched in greeting. She embraces Duncan briefly before extending her hand to take mine firmly, smiling ear to ear, and immediately launches into conversation.

'Has Duncan told you what's special about my room here at Newnham?' she asks. I look questioningly first at Duncan and then at her, shaking my head. 'Well, look around you', she says. 'This room belonged to Germaine Greer! In fact, the striped green wall paper you see on the walls was her pick and, some say, put up by her with her own hands! The upholstery on the sofa too was her selection, and I've left it as I found it. So basically, I haven't changed a thing since I moved in here after her'. She continues, not stopping for a pause, 'You see that chest before the fireplace? Well, they'd blocked the fireplace a long time ago and had electrical wiring installed in the chimneys, but when I moved in, I found logs in this chest. Obviously, Germaine had decided to have a log fire in her room, electrical wiring notwithstanding!' I'm stunned as she bursts out laughing, and immediately, I feel a strong affinity with her. I extend the little silk pouch with earrings that I've brought her as a gift; and she instantly proceeds to remove her own and wear the new ones. I'm touched, even as Duncan flashes out his phone to take a picture of her with the new earrings. I also present them the bottle of Prosecco I've brought along as a family gift, and it's their turn now to be touched.

Soon, we're off to the Newnham faculty hall for lunch. It's a buffet laid out daily for faculty and guests in a grand and airy dining hall, with framed portraits of Newnham founder Henry Sidgewick and his wife, as well as of other dignitaries. Lunch is sumptuous, with soup, salad, vegetarian and meat dishes, a selection of cheese, crackers and fruit, and a dessert of churros (which I figure out are the Spanish version of doughnuts) with chocolate sauce.

Conversation at lunch is pleasant and effortless. We discuss my daughters; their childhoods and their marriage plans (of all the things!). Duncan and Sheila are intrigued by the tradition of arranged marriage in India, and they want to learn how the whole business of 'arranging' for a boy and a girl to marry each other is conducted. They're curious to know my own views on the matter, and are not a little astounded that I'm willing to flout this tradition and let my girls choose whoever they want to marry. On my part, I'm eager to find out more about the history and feminist leanings of Newnham; of how it has retained, and firmly positioned itself as a 'women only' institution when almost all of Cambridge has opened the doors of its previously 'men only' institutions to women. As we partake of the excellent fare, I notice two long tables in the hall being elegantly laid out for a meal, and I'm told that a few Dames, alumni of Newnham, (Emma Thompson among them) have been invited to dinner tonight. Sheila is pleasantly nonchalant about it, while I cannot restrain the awed expression on my face. I bend over my plate to conceal it. I'm sure Sheila has seen, but she's too gracious to reveal it; and it's alright. During the lunch, I notice both Duncan and Sheila being attentive to one another, asking if either wanted anything from the buffet, taking care to refill each other's glass of water. As they talk affectionately of their 14 year old son Michael, I can sense the strength of the bond that unites them. The traditional Indian woman in me looks for social sanction; and 'why they haven't married' is a question I'll probably end up asking Duncan later if the occasion permits. The conversation veers towards British colonialism, and about how so many of the artefacts finding pride of place in British museums and institutions are nothing but the loot of empire. I nod my head, and when Sheila suggests that ideally, Britain should return the artefacts we're talking about, I gently reply that if Britain were indeed to do that with every object they acquired during the heyday of the Empire, most British museums would be rendered empty! Amidst the laughter generated, we go off with Sheila to visit the Newnham library.

The library at Newnham is a gracious, well-lit room, with an old section – the ceilings of which are done up in a gorgeous azure blue with white plaster friezes; and a new addition where the architect has retained the colour scheme and general layout of the old, investing it with an appearance that makes it look organically connected to the original. Sheila is full of anecdotes about the library. As we cross a room, I notice two carved wooden corner pieces on each side of the door, and remark that they look Indian to me. 'Oh, loot!' whispers Sheila conspiratorially, and we break into suppressed giggles. Five generations down, she does not feel any guilt, just as I do not feel any rancour. It hits me suddenly, that this, this absence of anger or bitterness has more or less characterised my reaction towards the people I have met in Britain. They've all been enormously friendly and generous. I've not encountered any racism. I've asserted my pride in my nationality, without undermining their pride in theirs. It's 70 odd years down the line anyway, and the tables have turned. Dramatically so, with India on the road to being the next superpower, and Britain quite clearly on the back-foot as it negotiates its new found isolation in the wake of Brexit. The tour is soon over, and we bid goodbye to Sheila, but not before I've asked her to join me for lunch at least once before I leave for India, for which she cheerfully agrees. I know that I will remember her always, this smiling, happy partner of Duncan, so clearly and obviously in love with him, so warm and affable, so unaffected by her visibly snooty position, and so willing to give!

As soon as we're back in the car again, I blurt it out, 'I can see exactly what you saw in Sheila, Duncan. She's a wonderful woman, so full of the joy of life!' Duncan smiles warmly as he concurs. Then we're off for the highlight of the day, punting down the river Cam![1] The day is gloriously sunny, speckled with a few classic British clouds; the river is magically quiet as there are not many punts around. Duncan steers the boat expertly as I look around all agog, taking in the view of the 'Backs', as they're known here, of the various Cambridge colleges. Duncan makes for a distinctive punter, a

1 Boating on the river Cam is done in narrow long boats that are propelled not by oars, paddles or motor, but by long poles (quants) held by the boatman who stands at the narrow end of the boat, inserts the pole all the way down to the river bottom, and propels the boat forward by pushing off the river bed. The task requires expertise and skill.

university professor in formal shirt and tweed coat, looking for all he's worth, like a gondolier with a PhD. We pass under bridges, one after the other: the Mathematical Bridge (made without nuts and bolts), the Bridge of Sighs (made to mirror the one in Venice), and the original Cam-Bridge, the first bridge across the river. At some point, Duncan accidently drops his punt pole into the river, and has to paddle (with his hands) back and forth to retrieve it. 'A first!' he quips. Not a minute later, we come across another punt full of tourists, sitting with a professional punter who has *also* dropped his punt pole. He stands at the edge of the boat, covertly wringing his hands in despair while trying to appear nonchalant as he waits for someone to retrieve his punt pole for him. Once again, we go paddling back and forth as Duncan plays the knight in shining armour, managing to rescue the pole and deliver it into the hands of the hapless pro. Then we're off again, gliding down the gentle Cam as Duncan gives me trivia about the places we're crossing. Autumn reveals itself in all its resplendent colours, the river banks are quiet, and Cambridge passes by in all its elegant beauty. The hour is soon up, the punt must be returned, and we're ready for the next step of this tour.

But first, it has to be a cup of tea. A pot of Assam tea, no less, and an indulgent scone (my throwback to Enid Blyton) later, we're off again, I want to shop for Cambridge Tshirts for my girls, and Duncan readily obliges, taking me to two or three shops before I finally make up my mind. I don't know it yet, but he's also bought me a souvenir; a fridge magnet depicting a punt as it sails down the Cam, the punter steady with the punt pole. 'A little memory of today', he smiles as he puts it in my hands. I'm too overwhelmed to react in any other way except with a 'Thank You'. It's already dark at 4.45 pm as we make our way to King's College Chapel for Evensong.[2] This will be the third Evensong I'll have attended during my British sojourn, Exeter and Canterbury being the other two.

King's College was established by Henry VI in 1441. Its Chapel is one of Britain's most iconic buildings, standing graceful and majestic, unharmed even after the ravages of the two world wars. I am awed as I take in its elegantly imposing fan vaulted stone ceiling; but what

2 The evening prayer service in church, conducted musically in many cathedralsespecially of the Anglican Church. It consists of prayers, psalms and canticles chanted according to a set form.

really catches my eye is a painting at the far end of the chapel that is mounted where the altar should be. It's an original Rubens – *The Adoration of the Magi*, done in magnificent reds. As I allow the significance of this painting used as an altarpiece, to sink in, Duncan gently leads me to our seats, as the chapel seems to be filling up rapidly with attendees. They're mostly tourists, I spot quite a few Chinese among them, who are as goggle eyed as I am with the splendor of this place. To think that all of this belongs to an educational institution! The service begins, and as I attune my ears to symphonic rise and fall of voices singing in unison, I realise with a start that they're not singing to any accompaniment. There's no church organ playing today, yet I don't feel the lack of a musical instrument. The choir is in complete harmony, the voices are clear, clean, and melodious, rising and falling like the crest and trough of a wave in low tide, lulling one to a sense of calm repose. My convent school background makes me familiar with some of what they sing, and for the rest, there are handouts given to the attendees so they can follow. When it ends, I open my eyes with a sigh. Duncan's looking at me, 'Does that to you, doesn't it?' he smiles as we walk out of the chapel into a dark night at 6 pm.

The last stop for the day is dinner at Carluccio's with Michael, Duncan and Sheila's teenaged son. Duncan lets on that it's their family's favourite restaurant, and they dine here frequently. We take our seats and wait for Michael to arrive from a music lesson. I am told that he's learning to play the clarinet, and will be sitting for the Trinity school music exams soon. But this, it turns out, is only one of the many accomplishments of the tall, charming, young boy who walks into the restaurant just a few minutes later, embraces his father, and extends his hand to me saying, 'Hi, I'm Michael.' As we settle down and wait for our orders to arrive, I learn more about him. He's a polyglot, I soon discover, and learns Judo otherwise. He's fond of traveling, and finds classes in school boring (now where have I heard that before?). He's easy to talk to and eager to listen, well mannered, and attentive. I can see that he has the perfect mix of his parents; his father's boyish charm and his mother's sense of humour, in addition to being supremely talented, like them. I observe how proud Duncan is of his son, how he listens carefully to Michael, nodding his head and laughing when he senses a joke. Dinner accomplished, we wish bye-bye to Michael as he heads off for a game of football on his bicycle. Cycling is how they move around in both Cambridge and

Oxford, especially the students, and not a few university dons. The image of a student in flowing robes rushing for class on his 'flying' bicycle is an iconic Oxbridge image, one that I carry back home with me imprinted on both a fridge magnet and a mug.

It's a beautiful, affectionate family I have encountered today: close-knit, considerate, smiling, and happy. I feel fuzzy in my heart. Something like tears seems to be welling up inside. A sense of being blessed comes upon me; to have been a part of this experience at Cambridge, to have met and known this family, to have shared a brief moment of their life, their generosity, their goodness, their happiness. Duncan envelops me in a bear hug as we bid adieu at the train station. I thank him, excruciatingly aware all the while, that words are not enough to communicate what I feel. As if on cue, it begins to rain just as the train glides out of the platform. The sun was out for me today in usually rainy England. The showers held up all day, so that Cambridge could reveal itself to me in all its gracious beauty. I settle down on my seat, exhausted but content, as I send up to the heavens a silent prayer of gratitude, for the weather, for this day and this experience, for life.

CHAPTER 5

Children of America: Narrating the Transnational Experience in Jhumpa Lahiri's *Unaccustomed Earth*

Dr. Anita Luther Bhasin

Abstract

It is a recognised fact that the dominant trope that identified the diasporan was the archetypal exile of the Jews from Israel and the forced migration of the indentured labourers and its concomitant nostalgia for the homeland. However, in this globalised world interconnectivity through modern electronic communications systems, ease of travel and economic interfaces produced by multinational capital, the term "Diaspora" includes not only community dispersal but also any form of migration.

It follows that this new breed of voluntary migrants, the transnational migrants, so different from the disenfranchised exiles of old constitute the new phenomenon of the "transnation", go globe-hopping for education or bettering their economic prospects. The shock of displacement and sense of alienation still remains amongst the new first generation diasporans but their hyphenated children have adapted to their situation and embrace their multicultural identities, equally at ease in both worlds: American and Indian.

It is this experience and the inter-generational clashes that Jhumpa Lahiri explores in her second collection of short stories *"Unaccustomed Earth"*. In dealing with the metaphoric striking of roots deep into American soil, the stories go on to briefly delineate the struggles and process of acculturation of the parents and the easier integration of the children who embrace American values of individualism and freedom of choice in matters of love, marriage and careers. In portraying the everyday, universal experiences of the characters that populate these stories in this globalised world these "children of America" are the true transnationals taking on fluid identities. However, in so doing, Lahiri does not grapple with issues of racism and the tribalisation of cultural experiences which appears to be a lacuna with most diasporic writers.

Keywords: Diaspora, Transnational, Hyphenated Children, Displacement, Exile

Till the late twentieth century, the dominant trope that identified the diasporan was the archetypal exile of the Jews from Israel and the forced migration of the indentured labourers with its concomitant nostalgia for the homeland. Safran famously declared that they have "retained a memory of, a cultural connection with, and a general orientation towards their homeland culture and / or religion; they relate in some (symbolic or practical) way to their homeland; they harbor doubts about their full acceptance by the host land; they are committed to their survival as a distinct community, and many of them have retained a myth of return" (Safran 10). However, in this globalised world interconnectivity through modern electronic communications systems, ease of travel and economic interfaces produced by the multinational capital, cultural hybridity, once the hallmark of the diasporic condition, now pervades the world. It follows that the term 'Diaspora' includes not only community dispersal but also any form of migration. As a result of this paradigm shift, some Diaspora critics have started focusing more on the 'constructive potential' of Diaspora by viewing it as "mediating cultures"(Clifford 302-338) wherein migrants try to come to terms with their hybridized identity and multiple belongings (Tölölyan 3-36).

This is not to say that the shock of displacement and sense of alienation does not pervade the diasporic condition. It is still there amongst the new first generation diasporans but amongst their hyphenated children, the old pain of enforced assimilation has given way to joyous adaptation. This new breed of voluntary migrants, the transnationals as they are called, so different from the disenfranchised exiles and émigrés of old, constitutes the new phenomenon of the "transnation" (Ashcroft 68 1-1ff) as they globe-hop for education or economic betterment. It follows that the tropology of diaspora has shifted from the linear and temporal axis of irreversible departure from the homeland and host land in, for the fortunate, a borderless world.

Jhumpa Lahiri, in her second collection of short stories, *Unaccustomed Earth*, has gone beyond depicting the sense of shock and alienation amongst the first generation Bengali-Indian immigrants to focus on their hyphenated children. The title, borrowed from Nathaniel Hawthorne's "*The Custom House*", holds the key to understanding the stories and goes like this:

> Human nature will not flourish, any more than a potato, if it be planted and replanted, for too long a series of generations, in the same worn-out soil. My children have had other birthplaces, and so far as fortunes maybe within my control, shall strike their roots into Unaccustomed Earth.

This extract makes Lahiri's intentions clear as she goes on to delineate the intellectual invasion of America by the relatively affluent and highly educated Indian immigrants, who come to America to seek greener pastures, the pain of their acculturation and the easier integration of their children who are simultaneously American and Indian.

The idea of Bengali immigrants striking deep roots in American soil is reinforced in the titular first short story "Unaccustomed Earth", which also sets the tone of the rest of the stories. Ruma has faced a dislocation as she and Adam with Akash, their son, have moved from Brooklyn to Seattle. She gives up her part-time job in a law firm in New York and is now expecting her second child. She is lonely and misses her Brooklyn friends. Her recently widowed father has come to visit her. Torn between her duty of keeping him with her after her mother's death and in retaining her independence, she has mixed feelings about his visit. Her father, on the other hand, does not expect Ruma to keep him for she was "not raised with that sense of duty" (Unaccustomed Earth, 29). He has sold the big house in New York and has moved into a smaller apartment. In his innumerable travels post retirement, he has met a sixty year old widow, Mrs Bagchi and they carry on a discreet affair. Lahiri makes it clear that his involvement with Mrs Bagchi was not due to passion, but because he wanted companionship. She, on the other hand, did not want to marry because she "had loved her husband of two years more than he had loved his wife of nearly forty" (Unaccustomed Earth 40). This is a telling commentary on the state of his marriage. He had found his wife, who stuck to Indian attire and habits demanding, was oblivious to her needs but was a passionate gardener and had toiled in unfriendly soil, coaxing exotic Indian vegetables from the ground for his wife who missed them. When Ruma does finally extend her father the invitation to stay, he refuses because he prefers to keep his independence. Before going, he plants a hydrangea, a flower his wife liked. It did not prove that he loved or missed her but was his way of honouring her.

The points that emerge through the synoptic discussion of the story, reinforced in the other stories, are the process of acculturation of Ruma's parents; the independence and easier integration of the children who marry Americans, and the metaphoric interpretation of striking deep roots in American soil. Of course, keeping within the constraints of short stories, the process of acculturation has not been dealt with in detail. Nevertheless, the struggles of the parents remain in the background as they from their own enclaves and retain the customs and values of the homeland while negotiating their adjustments in the host country. In so doing, they are like the roots of the hydrangea penetrating deep into foreign soil that Ruma's father plants, making it possible for their children to flourish, just as Ruma, Adam, Akash and the unborn baby will be striking in a new place. This idea is contained in all the stories and the only exceptions are Amit's parents in "A Choice of Accommodations" and Kaushik's parents in the trilogy "Hema and Kaushik". They are well to do and can afford the luxury of shuttling back and forth from host land and to homeland. It also delineates the hardships they face, ensuring that their children flourish and also of their children negotiating their journeys through both worlds, by and large successfully, without encountering feelings of alienation.

What these stories make clear is that all the parents are successful because of their education. Moreover, there is there no sense of economic deprivation amongst them. In fact, they are viewed as a model minority who have a firm grasp of the English language, work hard and honour their elders. These qualities go a long way towards explaining why Indian-Americans have been so successful at attaining "middle and upper middle class status ... higher incomes and more secure careers" (Dhingra, 246). It is these values that they transmit to their children as they push them to achieve more. If they choose not to make a success of their lives, to fit into the mould their parents have cast for them, is also a part of the second generation Indian-American experience. Their decisions are governed by their right to make their own choices. In "Unaccustomed Earth" Ruma decides to give up her job as a lawyer and become a full-time mother. Her father voices his concern when he tells her, "It makes me nervous that you are not employed" (Unaccustomed Earth 38). Amit in "Choice of Accommodations" harbours a grudge against his parents for putting him in boarding school and feels abandoned. His parents want him to become a doctor; instead he chooses to work for a medical Journal. Sangeeta Biswas, Sang, in "Nobody's Business" is a Harvard dropout. Rahul in "Only Goodness" too drops out of college because of his alcoholism. It is his sister Sudha who has attained a double Masters and goes to LSE. Similarly, Hema in "Hema and Kaushik" has completed her Ph.D., and has a tenured position in a University. Kaushik is a successful photo-journalist. What must be noted is the priority parents place on education. They strive to give their children the very best. However, the children exercise their choice in either using their education to advance their goals and careers or abandon it for whatever reasons they give to justify their actions.

Generational and cultural clashes also take place between the parents and their children especially when it comes to marriage and love. In keeping with tradition, the parents enter into arranged marriages and the children become aware of the loveless state of their parents' marriages. Ruma's father had endured her resentment of his treatment of her mother not realising that her mother had been overly demanding. Sudha too is struck by the lack of emotion in her parents' marriage in "Hell-Heaven" which best deals with this aspect. It is a sensitive portrayal of Usha's mother trapped in a loveless marriage. Her father had married her mother to placate his parents. Her mother does not love her husband but is duty bound to continue with the marital ties. She is lonely and falls in love with Pranab Chakraborty. When he marries Deborah, an American, she is consumed with jealousy and tries to commit suicide. She only tells her daughter that years later when Usha's heart had been broken by a man she'd hoped to marry. What must be noted is that the first generation diasporans cling to homeland practices and traditions especially where marriage is concerned. The marital bonds are sacrosanct and its dissolution is not an option.

This is an unthinkable situation for the children who enter into relationships and who marry persons of their choice. Of course clashes take place, especially with the girls, who want to be given the freedom their American counterparts have. If acceptance comes, it comes reluctantly as Usha states, "Slowly she accepted that I dated an American man, and then another, that I slept with them, and even that I lived with one though we were not married. She welcomed my boyfriends into our home and when things didn't work out she told me I would find someone better" (Unaccustomed Earth 82). Ruma had kept her involvement with men a secret from her parents and until she announced her engagement to Adam. Her mother had tried her best to talk her out of it and accepts Adam as their son only after Akash's birth. Pranab Chakraborty and Amit go against their parents' wishes and marry American girls. Amit's mother reluctantly accepts Megan years later, a concession not accorded to Deborah. Sang carries on an affair with an Egyptian and spurns arranged marriages. Rahul decides to break off with tradition and moves in with an aspiring actress who has a daughter from a previous boyfriend. Sudha marries an Englishman, Roger Featherstone. Hema has broken off an affair with Julian because he refused to divorce his wife and marry her. Eventually she agrees to marry Navin because she could not face the prospect of approaching middle age without a husband and children. In her heart of hearts she knows that it is an arranged marriage, something she had spurned in the past. Navin is willing to make adjustments and to move to Massachusetts to be with Hema, something Kaushik would not have done. It is for this reason she refuses to accompany Kaushik into a romantic journey filled with uncertainties. Nevertheless, she does not hesitate to enter into an affair with him on the eve of her marriage which is an unthinkable act for the first generation parents.

In all these cases the children have exercised their choice in either choosing careers or partners for themselves which shows not only their growing independence but also the fact that they have accepted American values and traditions. Does this mean that because they inhabit multiple cultural spaces and belong nowhere that a sense of profound uncertainty is created? This does not happen to be the case especially for the hyphenated children and that "third space" (Bhabha 143) is not characterised by the state of unrelieved anxiety or despair. The Indian-American Diaspora in Lahiri's stories are to be found in multiple locations living their everyday lives, which could also be considered symbolic of the universal condition. The claims of nationality and culture are cast-off to allow for an exploration of new territories. These experiences of removal and distinction are shared alike by all the new Diaspora who is a global soul. As a result "the global soul draws its freedom from a sense of non-affiliation of being loosed from time as much as from space" (Jain 16). Jain goes on to say that the global soul has adapted to new technologies and globalisation, and is a nomad with no claim or affiliations to any country or space. They are "nowarians", to use Pico Iyer's term, who writes, "I had no history I could feel and lived under the burden of no home..." (Iyer23). Lahiri, who faces a similar situation, has used this situation to her advantage and revels in her multiple locations called home. This sense of exhilaration is conveyed in this collection of stories wherein the children are at ease in both worlds and negotiate their hyphenated existences with ease. The only character who can be given the dubious distinction of being a "nowarian" is Kaushik. I maintain that it is dubious because he is running away from his father's second family, his stepmother and his step sisters who are suffocatingly Indian to him. In this regard Stuart Hall's remark in his "Introduction; Who Needs Identity" is apt:

> ... (I)dentities are never unified and in late modern times, increasingly fragmented and fractured, never singular but multiple, constructed across different, often intersecting and antagonistic, discourses, practices and positions. They are subject to a radical historicisation and are constantly in the *process of change and transformation*...Identities are therefore constituted within, not outside representation (Hall 4. Italics mine).

Precisely because historicisation is a continuous process the reader finds that in this globalised world, the migrants take on a fluid identity and in the mosaic of cultures that is America these migrants are at home in both worlds. The first generation diasporans would like to carry on their homeland practices and perpetuate homeland values in their children and gradually, if reluctantly, accept the Americanisation of their children. As Usha in "Hell Heaven" aptly states, "My mother and I had also made peace; she had accepted the fact that I was not only her daughter but a child of America as well" (Unaccustomed Earth 81-82).

It is these children of America who are the true transnationals, equally at home in both worlds. In none of the stories is there a feeling of being outsiders and being uncomfortable with their identities. The process of assimilation and integration has led to a kind of territorialisation as the claims of nationality and culture are cast off to allow for an exploration of new territories. Lahiri straddles various cultures with ease and has a unique advantage of being both an insider and outsider. Much has been written about the tribalisation of culture amongst the diasporans wherein they shut their doors to intercultural exchanges and global understanding; who refuse to integrate into the mainstream and stubbornly continue with their homeland practices and create ethnic enclaves for themselves. *Unaccustomed Earth* does not display these characteristics as the characters that populate the stories carry on with their everyday lives. However, as has been correctly pointed out, Lahiri "avoids serious engagement with issues relating to racism, ethnicity, identity, and multi-culturalism and fails to get beyond photographic descriptions of some places of the host countries like markets, streets, and workplaces with occasional peeps into the life of the natives" (Kar94). And it is this lacuna that makes the transnational experience incomplete.

References

Ashcroft, Bill. "Globalisation, the Transnation and Utopia". *Narrating the (Trans) Nation: The Dialects of Culture and Identity.* (eds.) Krishna Sen and Sudeshna Chakravarty. Kolkata: Dasgupta and Company, 2008. 1-23. Print.

Bhabha, Homi K. *"The Location of Culture".* London: Routledge, 1994. Print.

Clifford, J. "Diasporas"*Cultural Anthropology* 9.3 (1994). 302-338. Print.

Dhingra, Pawan. *"Managing Multicultural Lives Asian American Professionals andthe Challenge of Multiple Identities".* Stanford: Stanford University Press, 2007. Print.

Hall, Stuart and Paul Du Gay. "Introduction: Who Needs "Identity"?" *Questions of Cultural Identity.* (eds.) Hall and Du Gay. London: Sage Publications, 1996. 3-17. Print.

Iyer, Pico. *The Global Soul.* London: Bloomsbury, 2000. Print.

Jain, Jasbir. "Overwriting Memory: The Diaspora and Its Present" *Contemporary Indian Diaspora: Literary and Cultural Representations.* (ed.) AngshumanKar: Jaipur and New Delhi, 2015. 13-28. Print.

Kar, Angshuman. "Interrogating the 'Other' in Contemporary Indian Diaspora Fiction". *Contemporary Indian Diaspora: Literary and Cultural Representations.* (ed.) Angshuman Kar: Jaipurand New Delhi, 2015. 90-101. Print.

Lahiri, Jhumpa. *Unaccustomed Earth.* New Delhi: Random House, 2008. Print.

Safran, William. "Deconstructing and Comparing Diasporas". *Diaspora, Identity and Religion: New Directions in Theory and Research.* (eds.) Waltrand Kokot, Khachig Tölölyan and Carolin Alfonso. London: Routledge, 2004. 9-29. Print.

Tölölyan, Khachig. "The Nation-State and Its Others: In Lieu of a Preface". *Diaspora* 1.1 (1991). 3-7. Print.

CHAPTER 6

Searching for Selfhood in V.S. Naipaul's *India: A Wounded Civilisation*

Dr. Anoopama Yadav

Abstract

Expatriate writing occupies an eminent status between cultures and countries. It creates theory and determines positions as it posits a new individuality that confers boundaries and limits and brings into relation various temporal and spatial metaphors. The arts, customs, lifestyles, background, and habits characterise a particular society or nation and travel, take root or get dislocated. Individuals incorporate nostalgia into themselves. They may go through a loss of memory or forgetfulness. Authors living in foreign land continuously evolve cultural theories. This is possible as they are living on the margins of two societies. This expatriate apparition serves together and provides information related to background and foreground to their readers. V.S. Naipaul possesses a triple identity, as a West Indian, English, and Indian. This complexity is visible in his writings. He is the product of western culture and education. His work India: A Wounded Civilisation is a work of astonishing introspection and brilliance. While entailing about India, the land of his ancestors, Naipaul projects his wounded feelings and bitter realisation of his roots. In this paper, the selfhood of displaced Naipaul is seen in the context of cultural identity theory postulated by Stuart Hall.

Keywords: Expatriate, Selfhood, Identity, Culture.

Vidyadhar Suraj Prasad Naipaul was born in Chaguanas, Trinidad in 1932. He is an Indian Brahmin dislocated from the land of his ancestors and has a composite personality. A hundred years ago, his grandfather migrated to Trinidad as an indentured labourer. Naipaul, one of the pioneering, controversial, and best writers, was born in an impoverished rural Hindu-speaking area of Trinidad. He is a self-made exile. He lived as an expatriate in London. He is regarded as one of the greatest Caribbean writers in English. He is an eminent novelist and travel writer. Most of his writings interpret his departure from Trinidad to England.

India has always provided a recurring source or topic for V.S. Naipaul. As a novelist, he has put himself in jeopardy by looking into India with a western outlook. Naipaul is an unsatisfied Trinidad Indian. He visits India with the western eye of superiority. He observes and writes about India almost in a mental or emotional state of disregard, and aggressive inclination. He carries a payload of the adverse judgment formed beforehand without the knowledge of facts and fright of complexes.

Travelogue is a piece of writing about travel (merriam-webster.com). It is an account of an individual experience related to travelling. It is generally narrated in the past tense and the first person. The word travelogue comes from the combination of the two words travel and monologue. The word monologue is of Greek origin meaning *Monos* i.e. alone. *Logus* means speech. The essential component of travelogue comprises what the traveller sees, hears, tastes, smells, and feels in the world of his exploration. Through the travelogues, we come to explore the thought processes reflecting the writer's inner world. In one way, travelogues help in the revelation of the author's personality, inner thoughts, imagination, and expressiveness. The author informally conveys the information that he observes relating to travel which involves spatial displacement. Writers from different occupations, temperaments, ages, and climes have produced travel writing. Such writings have linkages with history, exploration, adventure, elements of autobiography, and experience-related revelation of the writer's personality. Travelogues also reveal the degree of writer's subjectivity or objectivity, their attitude towards the life of the people they travelled among.

Travelogues written by Naipaul are The Middle Passage, "India" Trilogy.

1. An Area of Darkness
2. India: A Wounded Civilisation
3. India: A Million Mutinies Now

The trilogy thus is not entirely a record of Naipaul's perception having a basis on his own acquired knowledge, opinion as an alien in exile. It is also a commentary on different themes about India that Naipaul believes important to wonder about.

India: A Wounded Civilisation is the second book in V.S. Naipaul's acclaimed Indian Trilogy. The book entails man's complex relationship with the country of his ancestors. The book is divided into three parts:

1. A Wounded Civilisation,
2. A New Claim on the Land,
3. Not Ideas, but Obsessions.

This book is a collection of eight essays in three parts, on his observation and experiences about India, during the internal emergency(1975-1977). With this intellectual understanding at one's disposal, though impolite and rough from the outlook of an average Indian, these essays yield good critic on life during the emergency period and Indian democracy in general.

Naipaul acknowledges his exceptional fixation on India. But in his books, his frame of mind is seen as British even so he is West Indian by birth and upbringing. This emotional artistic awareness which can be suitably termed as "expatriate sensibility" has made his position, his outlook faulty. He visited India during the emergency in 1975 when Mrs. Indira Gandhi was prime minister. This piece of work has received much critical acclaim. It is an outcome of a journey to search his roots. Naipaul witnessed and acquainted confrontations with Indians from a contemptuous indifferent Prince to an engineer building houses for the homeless. He has recorded India's diverse perplexity. Naipaul has stated about the emergency in his book. He says that his book entails-

> "An inquiry about India-even an inquiry about the emergency-has quickly to go beyond the political. It has to be an inquiry about Indian attitudes; it has to be an inquiry about the Civilisation itself, as it is." (IWC, 9)

This is reflected as the main motive of the book. He displays the religious customs of Aryans ironically, which were being followed by his family members, though they had left their Indian roots a century ago. At another instance, Naipaul says-

> "A hundred years had been enough to wash me clean of many Indian religious attitudes; and without these attitudes the distress of Indian was – and is – almost insupportable." (IWC, 9)

Naipaul has failed to acknowledge the holiness and the goodness of the Indian religion to be trifling. He is raised in a homogeneous community of Hindu indentured labourers in Trinidad. He concedes as true of having washed of practices or rituals of the religious beliefs. Knowledge of religious beliefs is necessary for comprehending Indian civilisation. Naipaul, being an outsider in India, regards the culture of India as foreign and believes that the customs and traditions have elevated frustration in him. It was very difficult for him to get scot-free himself even after his return to England. He deliberately did not pay attention to syncretism or different systems and beliefs of India, its varied art forms like music, classical dance, etc. Naipaul does not witness much in them as he is not proficient in any Indian language required to deeply probe in understanding classical Indian art forms. Howsoever, what makes Naipaul distinct is that his rejections are magnificently constructed. His connection with India is a way of interacting with his own past. One finds faults because one is concerned.

In mysteriously unsettling, primitive India, with its undeveloped status that Naipaul is aversive of – is what in present-day Western Europe is termed as sustainable living. Through writings on the ancestral homeland, Naipaul has ripped through the Indian psyche obstinately and pragmatically. For him, India is a difficult country. He has an explicit difficulty that has to be Indian part of his selfhood and he likely feels assaulted by it. He resolves in expressing 'they Indians' rather than 'We Indians'. He has portrayed the dark picture of his ancestral homeland. To him, India has failed as an independent country and its state or condition is too old for its people to advance. He would usually deform the state of affairs on the contrary making it clear; put in the unexpected phrases like 'Hindu way of life' to prove his point. He holds to account what he calls 'Hindu way of life' which in itself is the consequence of his Oriental's perspective. It is invidious to call a multi-secular country or its people 'Hindu'. Hinduism has become the reason for India's lacking sentiment, stimulation, powerlessness, and decaying through stillness, without progress or change. Moreover, the colonial inferiority of Indians is another cause of India's bewilderment disarray, and aimlessness which has finally wounded India's civilisation.

The caste system is prevalent in India. Untouchables are still supposed as impedance in the way of India's development. In some communities, the hierarchy between low caste and high caste, rich and poor, child marriage, and puberty marriage is still in practice. Major issues of modern India are crime, juvenile delinquency, and unrest among youths, and the sufferings of the aged people. Moreover, polygamy and polyandry system is still practiced in Toda,

Kota, and the Nair community. This has shattered the elevated image of India before the world. The prevalence of the sati system in the Hindu religion is regarded as the glory of Hinduism. In the same way, the talaq system is practiced among Muslims. These practices are obsolete, old-fangled, embarrassing, and primeval. Therefore, the Indian civilization goes along with the number of losses, lack of order and discombobulating. Hindu-Muslim riots, disharmony among different religions in India for the sake of religious identity, rituals, and norms have drifted the nation into disorder.

Naipaul's novel India: A Wounded Civilisation projects ubiquitous wounds and the pain people bear in independent India. All the eight essays covering this book were published about 40 years ago. Their significance is still visible today in India. Bonded labour or slavery is still seen, the caste system also prevalent and it is increasing in stature as well as flourishing. In the rural areas, poverty is seen. The problem with India from these essays is your cast defines who you are. There is no real way to escape it. It determines your place in society and status in the community. Naipaul gives an illustrative view of India through the lens of 'Oriental fatalism'. He never desists to observe. He finds fault in the psychology of Hinduism from the outlook of someone who is culturally Hindu himself. Though dislocated, he engrosses in his usual stubborn ideas or opinion and provides lacerating observations. A major portion of this book is devoted to a discussion on Indian religion and philosophy. All failures the country had passed through to date could be traced back to the failure of its comprehensive system of belief. Hinduism was a rudimentary religion and had depleted its usefulness. It had come to such a stage on account of resistance in the growth of religion. It supported self-complacency, idleness, passiveness, and repetition. Its philosophy supported stagnancy and inactivity, which made growth and enlargement impossible. Naipaul quotes examples of a Hindu comprehensive system of belief in self-absorption that is overly concerned about oneself, to the point of ignoring the feelings of others. He makes use of literature by Indian writers like R.K. Narayan and U. Krishnamurthy, to emphasise the voluntary destructiveness of the religion. Hindu religion devised different activities on which an individual's whole state of health, happiness, and prosperity depended upon. It was the country's bad luck that its religion was responsible for retarding its growth and promoted withdrawal. It is based on the doctrine that all events are subject to faith or inevitable necessity, or determined in advance in such a way that human beings cannot change them. Its fatalism was instrumental of enumerated defeats and damage, and even though the philosophy of the Hindu religion of ongoingness, continence promised its renewal of vigor and vitality time and again. It was renewed without in-look or change. Indian philosophy had not only paved the way for colonialism, but it has also admitted and recorded it. Indians had become adept at self-deceit and self-delusion and lived with the faith or mental acceptance that all was well, no endeavor was needed, and that it would proceed to remain alive. The country's vulnerability and pillage at the hands of Muslim invaders and later the British merchants of East India Company were of their own making upheld by an incurious, indifferent, and impassive religion. Hinduism had comprehended and embraced within its boundary more than it could maintain and the country was paying the price of its insufficiency and lack of competency.

> "Hinduism hasn't been good enough for the millions. It has exposed us to a thousand years of defeat and inactivity. It has given men no idea of a contract with other men, no idea of the state. It has enslaved one-quarter of the population and always left the whole fragmented and vulnerable. Its philosophy of withdrawal has diminished men intellectually and not equipped them to respond to challenge; it has stifled growth. So that, again and again in India history has repeated itself vulnerability, defeat, withdrawal."(IWC,43)

Naipaul believes that the civilisation of India is wounded. Western technological superiority and dominance have weakened her. He opined that intellectual Hindu Civilisation has been dominated for too long first by the Muslim invasions and later by the Britishers. There are wounds apparent in the emotions, attitudes, and consciousness of the people. He even goes to the anarchy of naming Muslim rulers as foreigners, even though when most are staying for many centuries and never left India. Naipaul doesn't want to be known as Indian when his ancestral roots belong to India and his ancestors have been out of India for hundred years. He objects by raising an eyebrow when some Muslim tells him that his family is residing in India for the last five centuries. In his view, all the last thousand years of the country are 'dark ages'. He regards himself to be of the new world.

In the book, Naipaul concentrates on the history of the conquest of India at the hand of forces from outside, more specifically the Mughals. India has never overcome the plunder of the Muslim invasions and colonialist strategies of the British. This was predictable or impossible to avoid because Indian civilisation was not sufficient and not heeded to its interests. The book makes cutting remarks on the long-term damage on Hindu philosophy, it has caused to the country. Sites of Hindu culture such as the kingdom of Vijayanagar and the historical region of Bundi – Kota in Rajasthan, are perceived as symbols of failure of the Indian comprehensive system of beliefs, and repeated records of invasion by foreigners witness to the weakness of Indian culture in sustaining its civilisation. Naipaul believes in 'A Wounded Civilisation', that the present crisis India faces on account of its being unable to survive the intellectual and creative exhaustion brought on by Muslim invasions. The history of India has not a wonderful history but it is a record of countless defeats.

Colonial inferiority of Indians is another reason for India's discombobulation and lack of clarity or order. The presence of British in India from the early seventeenth century to mid-twenties cause serious loss in the arena of customs, traditions, rituals, religion, polity, and economy and terrain of the country. The nation then went into the hands of the outsiders. It was the commencing of the defeat of political nationhood of the Indians in India. The country is consistently under distressing events of one kind or the other. This emotional wound doesn't give Indians any time to consider and think objectively. Naipaul has uncovered the reality which is filled with chaos and without the sense of historical continuousness. He analyses the Indian psyche and identifies precisely the incoherent and vague thinking and mythologising that is commonly widespread in the intellectual life of India. The novel could be seen as a review of the moral discernment; mental darkness of Indians to the real world who choose ignorance and heedlessness to live and evaluate themselves and others through the myopic glass of perceived high culture of centuries of rich civilisation.

Naipaul writes in the very first lines about the climatic conditions of India. Viewing fellow visitors at the airport makes him believe that India is at the edge of the Arabian world as it was in the 8th century. He believes that India has shrunk after the Arab incursion. India never shrunk rather it sailed continuously overseeing all the hurdles. He pinpoints the failure of India to overcome the conquest of foreigners. Naipaul holds that no civilisation in the world is ill-equipped like India to cope up with foreign invasions. The number of pillage seen by Indian civilisation is far more than any other in this world. Yet, it could not learn lessons from failures in the past. Naipaul explores the reasons responsible for the present situation of India. Through his artistic, articulated writings he focuses on men and sights to tell about the present condition of India and the consequences. He shares an account of his meeting a gentleman named Qureshi a Muslim, as he landed in Bombay, India. He comes to know that the Muslim guy is serving in the Indian Administrative Services. It puzzles him. But for an average Indian, this account is not that important as it was made significant by Naipaul. Later, he moves on to the topic of industrialisation in modern India. He tells that rapid advancement in science and technology and vital steps taken under the five-year plans have made India progress in different fields. It has become the world's fourth-largest grain producer.

Naipaul misinterprets the concept of Dharma. It means that one should be devoted to his duty and worship it. A person while performing his duty should not interfere in other people's duty unless it is needed. Naipaul is unable to understand this concept. We see flavor of pessimism in the following lines:

> "The crisis of India is not political. This is only the view from Delhi. Dictatorship or rule by the army will change nothing. Nor is the crisis only economic. These are only aspects of the larger crisis, which is that of decaying civilisation, where only hope lies in further swift decay."(IWC, 174-175)

In the introductory essay, he correlates his Indian visit with the details assimilated from the novel 'Mr Sampath' (1947) of Indian writer R.K. Narayan. Later he aligns his experience with the constant invasions of land in past and its propensity to answer by moving back to archaism. It has no alternative for modernity like court, parliament, and press.

Naipaul holds a negative perspective related to Gandhism. He opines:

> "Gandhi swept through India, but has left it without an ideology. The awakened the Holy land; is Mahatma good returned it to archaism; he made his worshippers vein."(IWC, 146)Naipaul asserts many deficiencies in the vision of Gandhi, father of the nation. Gandhi lost relevance after independence as the society resorted towards disharmony and fissiparous tendencies. Gandhi was successful in uniting people to obtain the goal of gaining independence. Once the country became free from foreign rule, Gandhi was given iconic status and forgotten. He is seen as a failure in inculcating the feeling of unity among his countrymen. After independence, his philosophy could not get solve the problems faced by

the people. His philosophy could not solve problems related to the threat of war from neighbouring countries, issues related to industrialisation, and the disintegration of family and community. No one practices the ideals given by Gandhi. He remains in the memory of people and his ideals are used for propaganda by Gandhian's when the need arises. The majority of Gandhi followers joined the Congress party after independence making it difficult for other national parties to match or exist in the same level with the Congress party. As a result, continuous victory in elections has made Congress a corrupt party steeping the nation into an ambiguous state of mental and moral depression. Naipaul opines:

"The stability of Gandhian India was an illusion; and India will not be stable again for a long time. But in the present uncertainty and emptiness there is a possibility of a true new beginning, of the emergence in India of the mind, after the long spiritual night." (IWC, 161) Gandhi is like a grotesque misrepresentation now, making inferior spiritualists like Vinoba Bhave a chance to strengthen themselves with his reflected honor; and immoral politicians to demand themselves as his followers.

The western hegemony is also instrumental to India's wounded civilisation. West is sequentially represented as superior whereas East as inferior. The East is seen as sensual, irrational, and primitive. One is made to believe that India being wounded by many centuries of foreign rule has not yet discovered a doctrine of spiritual rebirth or is unable in spontaneous restoration. West is regarded as rational, civilised, progressive, and so on. In this way, the West is always seen as the center and the East as marginalised. The discourses created by colonisers about the East make use of another basic opposition that the West is disciplined, enlightened, rational, and entrepreneurial whereas the East is passive, savage, and undisciplined. The self-assurance of colonisers is further hindered by what Bhabha calls mimicry – somewhat alien and deformed way – to which the colonised under threat or compulsion will imitate the coloniser's ways and expressions. V.S. Naipaul has painted characters in this book that have similar feelings of Western hegemony. They are unable to resist. He views that India has not been able to grow by herself. She hasn't found her own philosophy of restructuring. India is submerged in mimicry within mimicry.

Naipaul reproduces the convincingly happy and peaceful world of his childhood but is it is only an old childhood Hindu world he can joyfully connect to. This world envisages up again when he goes on a Yatra to the shrine of Shiva at Amarnath. He summarises experiences of safety and cheerfulness of belonging to a country and having a home when his Brahmin sensitivity relates his experiences in India to what he had witnessed as a boy in Trinidad. During these moments, Naipaul is ready to remain open to the presence of the country. But when he is not confronted with familiar awareness of childhood, he intends to attack India with western predisposition and partiality. Naipaul sees deep defects in contemporary Indian culture and goes on to track the lineage of these defects in Hindu religion and history. He claims that these flaws still exercise the ordinary Indian mind. One of Naipaul's major findings is that Indian people are neither hardworking nor do they have apprehension of the real world. Whenever they face a crisis, they take a resort to their glorious past and withdraw from the immediate world.

It would be foolish to dismiss his work as he tells a lot of truth about India. However, what is so annoying about the book is that he does not see anything good or important in India's present. He decries the country's lack of originality, its blind approval, and imitation of western thought in science and technology, art, and architecture. Lack of intellectual originality influenced Indian scholars as well, and irrespective of whether the Western Ideas matched the biasness and fore conceived mental apprehension about the country and its people. Subsequently, he is not able to gain aspects of the Indian outlook on their culture, religion and recognise or proclaim these variations of perception as differences necessarily cropping out of different cultural experiences. Aimlessness and lack of clarity and order are seen in people's way of thinking and working. This thought has aroused great crisis in the culture of India. He opines that India has not been able to change and to bring into her philosophy that would give rise to differentiate her from the mimicry of the west. He believes that intellect in India is of the second rate and all advancement is near imitation and mimicry of the West. India is still flagging from weakness. She is passing through illiteracy, poverty, backwardness, and centuries of British rule in India had adversely affected the culture, economy, and civilisation.

There are wounds in the mental state and consciousness of people. These crises and losses lead to the issue of selfhood and complicacy. What is identity? It is a very composite and indescribable and non-crystalline term that takes all the facets of culture, ancestral language, nation, and politics. It is not natural rather a created feature that can determine who we are simply. At the individual level, identity answers the query, who am I? And in the social context who are we in relation to other people. It is a concept of consciousness and not the inactive favor of history. A person's identity is the total of situations and experiences, nature and keeps on varying with time and space. It shows images not only of the past but paves roads to the future. Hence, it is not a right and fixed thing rather a fluid active procedure. Due to his lost identity and double alienation, Naipaul depicts a negative picture of India in his writings. His confused identity and confusion regarding his roots have contributed a lot to the negativity.

Stuart hall defines:

> "Identity is a matter of becoming as well as 'being. It belongs to the future as much as to the past. It is not something which already exists, transcending place, time, history, and culture, cultural identities come from somewhere I have history but like everything, have histories, but like everything which is historical they undergo constant transformation."(112) Identity is dynamic, non – static, and constantly changes, the ethnics go through diverse mental and emotional conflicts. They mainly have to face social problems of being inferior to the natives of the host land. Thus, the puzzling circumstances of alienation influence their consciousness. Due to the recollection of the past economic inequality, their visible state of being in their homeland and the logical negation of being somebody in their place generate the loss of Identity. Vijay Mishra calls this loss a psychology of dislocation. (123)

In his book India: A Wounded Civilisation Naipaul writes:

> "India is for me a difficult country. It isn't my home and cannot be my home; and yet I cannot reject it or be indifferent to it; I can't travel only for the sights. I am at once too close and too far."(IWC, 8)

Naipaul is bewildered and reveals it in his own words. He is in a puzzling circumstance and is not able to resolve anything with certainty whether India is his home or not. Naipaul proves himself to be as masterly in decoding secondary sources as he is proficient in carefully manipulating the crux out of first-hand experiences. It is less astonishing that he rebukes the Indians for their failure in vision. Once one actualises how weird insightful Naipaul himself is in the way he observes small things, in the way he brings together those with other time in particulars he has experienced, and in the way he draws inferences from this that is both astonishing and irresistibly evoking interest, presenting them in a marvelous language that is both consistent, accurate, and clear.

Naipaul's pessimistic writing depicts as if India will cease to exist within a short period. India is indeed a wounded civilisation but Naipaul in place of taking a position in healing this wound through his writing tries to hurt even more. He tries to follow everything negatively and writes in non – affirmative way. Some writers write negatively as they believe that by writing negatively and by creating strife they can gain popularity. It is well known that Naipaul has a large number of readers from all over the world especially the West. His writings are seen as a masterpiece and opinion or concept about the East is made according to what he writes. If he welcomes controversies by writing negative aspects about his ancestral homeland there are going to be more debates on what he says, thus increasing his fame in the Western world. Naipaul's delineation of India is not accepted by the majority of Indians. His depiction of India as a 'wounded civilisation' is imperfect. In a sense it is unrealistic. The reasons are crystal clear.

However, it must be said that what Naipaul writes about India is not completely untrue. He declared that India is crushed by restraining foreign rule and its shortcomings are acceptable. The author puts the responsibility of the country's backwardness on its religion and false apprehension of ancient glory. Naipaul had displayed the clash occurring out of cultural interpretations between him and the rest of India on every imaginable and possible aspect.

References

Bhabha, H. *The Location of Culture.*Routledge, London, 1994, pp. 1-122.

Hall, Stuart "Cultural identity and diaspora." *Jonathan Rutherford (ed.), Identity: Community, Culture Difference,* Lawrence and Wishart, London, 1998, pp. 110-237.

"Defination of Travelogue." *www.merriam-webster.com,* https://www.merriam-webster.com /dictionary/travelogue, Accessed 10 July 2021.

Mishra,V.(2007)."Traumatic Memory, Mourning and V.S.Naipaul. "*The Literature of Indian diaspora",* Routledge, 2007, pp. 106-132.

Naipaul, V.S. *India: AWounded Civilisation.* Picador, New York, 1977.

"What is a Travelogue." www.travelwritingworld.com, https://www.travelwriting world.com/what-is-a-travelogue, Accessed 10 July 2021.

CHAPTER 7

Decoding the Effect of Cultural Dimensions on Global Forms of Travel and Tourism

Anshuman Singh Chauhan

Abstract

One of the best ways to decode the way world functions cross border and achieve a harmoniously aligned functioning as one, is to look at it through the lens of Cultural Dimensions. Although, there exist multiple models to gauge such parameters, Geert Hofstede's Cultural Dimensions study relates to it the most. The very nature of these dimensions make them scalable with prospects of adding newer ways of cultural explorations, but the basic six dimensions, namely "power distance index (pdi)", "individualism versus collectivism (idv)", "masculinity versus femininity (mas)", "uncertainty avoidance index (uai)", "long term orientation versus short term normative orientation (lto)" and "indulgence versus restraint (ivr)" connect the best to the Global Forms of Travel & Tourism. This research paper aims to establish a causal connect between these six cultural dimensions presented by Hofstede and their effect on mindset, social cultural systems and perspectives of people hailing from different countries. It also intends to reflect travel patterns of people from different nationalities and their inferences of possible tourist destinations. Interestingly this paper reflects real life incidences and verbatims that convince the existing of research thoughts in reality.

Keywords: Cultural Dimensions, Global, Explorations, verbatims, Tourism.

With palms little sweaty, wrinkled forehead, brown shade of skin bent slightly towards dark tan, it was not tough for security staff at Sheremetyevo International Airport, Moscow to single me out as a suspicious nervous traveller. It was not first time for me travelling international, that too while travelling back home from a foreign country. The journey to New Delhi had typically, always seen me in thrills of all kinds, but this, was little different.

Three weeks back, placing myself comfortably over lunch table amongst my friends and colleagues in office, a simple disclosure of me travelling to India by a Russian carrier, had them in splits of laughter, eventually unboxing a range of perspectives through anecdotes and cultural legends. For next three week's literally till the day of my travel, my journey back home was hot topic of every leisurely discussion in office and outside. My regular lunch group had a beautiful mix and diverse range of people hailing from different countries and ethnicities. The perspectives they presented had a strong reflection of their cultural belief system, mixed with the experiences they gathered out of their journeys.

Over one of these discussions, 'Martin', my Danish friend &colleague, shared his concern over safety issues travelling with Russian carrier linking it with alcoholism, while' Eveline', who hailed from South Africa objected to the thought stating the Russian Carrier being operational since 1920's, holds most flying experience.US born 'Samantha', hadher thoughts liked to uncertainty of quality and performance, while my Indian friend 'Sumeeth' had his travels stories made possible due to carrier's low cost.

A week before my travel, on a fine Sunday while reflecting over past few weeks of diverse perspectives, concerns, critics, jokes, judgments and facts, compelled me to dig deeper into the subject of cultural dimensions, and during my research I bumped into a fine book titled *Cultures and Organisations*, authored by Geert Hofstede, Gert Jan Hofstede and Michael Minkov. Going through the detailed outlook presented with simplicity of cultural dimensions, I tried to run through the arguments presented by my friends and colleagues and look at them through the lens of these dimensions. To my surprise the dimensions as they are presented, provided a fine boundary for me to segregate all those arguments and decode them to build a firm understanding, linked to Travel & Cultural exchanges.

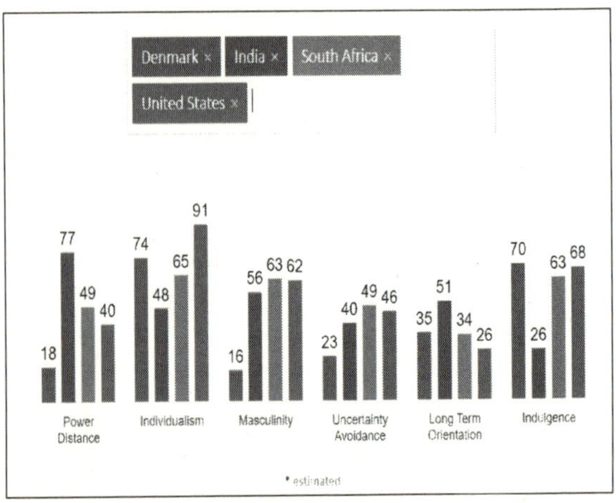

Courtesy: Hofstede-insights.com

Power Distance Index (Pdi)

This dimension expresses the degree to which the less powerful members of a society accept and expect that power is distributed unequally. People in societies exhibiting a large degree of Power Distance accept a hierarchical order in which everybody has a place, and which needs no further justification. In societies with low Power Distance, people strive to equalise the distribution of power and demand justification for inequalities of power.

A very strong reference to the impact could also be found in 2015 published study "The Impacts of Cultural Values on Bilateral International Tourism Flows" by scholars Yingsha Zhang, Tong (Stoltzer) Wu and Xiang (Robert) Li from University of South Carolina. This study explored the impacts of cultural values on international tourism flows. Agravity model for bilateral tourism flows was tested with data involving 81 original countries and 32 destination countries. The external validity of the model was examined by testing several sub-models for each destination. The results show that international tourists tend to flow from lower power distance countries to higher power distance countries.

The result from study, applied so very well to my set of friends and their travel history. Martin, who hailed from Denmark, had travelled the most amongst us and that too to the places that ranged from Far East and central Asian countries to central African ones, which usually do not fall on regular tourist map. US born Samantha, on other hand was an avid explorer of churches & museums and had already almost explored entire Europe during her early twenties. Eveline too had her share of travel history, which was mostly linked to countries in Africa and Middle East. She had her share of perspective that related to skin colour and country of origin that never encouraged her to explore much of western & European countries. While Sumeeth's history of travel was mostly linked to Work & Work related, and always had a component of cost linked to it. He hailed from India where power distance index is comparatively the highest.

Individualism versus Collectivism (Idv)

The high side of this dimension, called Individualism, can be defined as a preference for a loosely-knit social framework in which individuals are expected to take care of only themselves and their immediate families. Its opposite, Collectivism, represents a preference for a tightly-knit framework in society in which individuals can expect their relatives or members of a particular in group to look after them in exchange for unquestioning loyalty. A society's position on this dimension is reflected in whether people's self-image is defined in terms of "I" or "we."

As per the Zhang, Wu & Li 2015 study, the people in countries with a high level of individualism make more outbound trips, and these countries also receive more inbound travel. US & Western European countries present to us a classic case here. As per the report "India Tourism Statistics 2019" (Table 2.1.4), published on Govt. of India's tourism majority of travellers hail from North & South American OR Western & Eastern European countries, where most of the countries score very high on Individualism vs. Collectivism. Below is an extract of figures (between 2016-2018) on Nationality-Wise Foreign Tourist Arrivals in India:

TABLE 2.1.4

NATIONALITY-WISE FOREIGN TOURIST ARRIVALS IN INDIA, 2016-2018

Country of Nationality	Number of Arrivals			Percentage Share			Percentage Change	
	2016	2017	2018	2016	2017	2018	2017/16	2018/17
North America								
Canada	317239	335439	351040	3.6	3.34	3.32	5.7	4.7
U.S.A	1296939	1376919	1456678	14.73	13.72	13.80	6.2	5.8
Total	**1614178**	**1712358**	**1807718**	**18.33**	**17.06**	**17.12**	**6.1**	**5.6**
Central and South America								
Argentina	12308	14875	16345	0.14	0.15	0.15	20.9	9.9
Brazil	21289	24453	26579	0.24	0.24	0.25	14.9	8.7
Mexico	15689	18114	19909	0.18	0.18	0.19	15.5	9.9

Country of Nationality	Number of Arrivals			Percentage Share			Percentage Change	
	2016	2017	2018	2016	2017	2018	2017/16	2018/17
Others	29444	34625	38252	0.33	0.35	0.36	17.6	10.5
Total	**78730**	**92067**	**101085**	**0.89**	**0.92**	**0.96**	**16.9**	**9.8**
Western Europe								
Austria	33089	31832	33200	0.38	0.32	0.31	-3.8	4.3
Belgium	37960	41902	44086	0.43	0.42	0.42	10.4	5.2
Denmark	24717	26761	28195	0.28	0.27	0.27	8.3	5.4
Finland	18371	20384	21239	0.21	0.2	0.20	11	4.2
France	238707	249620	261653	2.71	2.49	2.48	4.6	4.8
Germany	265928	269380	274087	3.02	2.68	2.60	1.3	1.7
Greece	9048	10288	10658	0.1	0.1	0.10	13.7	3.6
Ireland	36440	37993	39276	0.41	0.38	0.37	4.3	3.4
Italy	95417	111915	126931	1.08	1.12	1.20	17.3	13.4
Netherlands	71840	76652	81615	0.82	0.76	0.77	6.7	6.5
Norway	20148	20882	22631	0.23	0.21	0.21	3.6	8.4
Portugal	54439	66378	74492	0.62	0.66	0.71	21.9	12.2
Spain	76342	81442	84356	0.87	0.81	0.80	6.7	3.6
Sweden	43889	45851	46743	0.5	0.46	0.44	4.9	1.9
Switzerland	48123	49607	49322	0.55	0.49	0.47	3.1	-0.6
U.K.	941883	986296	1029757	10.7	9.83	9.75	4.7	4.4
Others	13271	6492	15396	0.15	0.06	0.15	-51.1	137.2
Total	**2029412**	**2133673**	**2243635**	**23.05**	**21.26**	**21.25**	**5.1**	**5.2**
Eastern Europe								
Czech Rep.	12932	11852	13413	0.15	0.12	0.13	-8.4	13.2
Hungary	7961	9241	9201	0.09	0.09	0.09	16.1	-0.4
Kazakhstan	12979	15421	13314	0.15	0.15	0.13	18.8	-13.7
Poland	25706	28674	31565	0.29	0.29	0.30	11.5	10.0
Russian Fed.	227749	278904	262309	2.59	2.78	2.48	22.5	-6.0
Ukraine	26753	25988	26260	0.3	0.26	0.25	-2.9	1.0
Others	91922	102792	109997	1.04	1.02	1.04	11.8	7.0
Total	**406002**	**472872**	**466049**	**4.61**	**4.71**	**4.41**	**16.5**	**-1.4**

India, on the other hand, being more of a collective society presents a perfect setting for travellers from more Individualistic western societies to get a taste of community living, concept of society linked through a common ideology/religion and collective wisdom, represented boldly out through our festivities during festivals, weddings &prayer ceremonies, making us most sought after tourist destination in the world.

Masculinity versus Femininity (Mas)

The higher score on MAS dimension represents a preference in society for achievement, heroism, assertiveness, and material rewards for success. Society with higher degree on this dimension at large is more competitive. Its opposite, Femininity, stands for a preference for cooperation, modesty, caring for the weak and quality of life. Society at large is more consensus-oriented.

A deep dive into this dimension presents a huge contrast of how travel and its related industries get affected by the mere societal & cultural notion that a nation has to offer. For instance, a stag/solo travel opportunity to a Middle Eastern country would have less uptake by female travellers as compared to males, while if the opportunity originates from western / northern European country would see a higher traction from both the sexes. Although it would not be fair to put such a contrast out without it's due research, given forward looking country like Turkey presents a different perspective to far more judged middles eastern culture & it's effect on travel, thus it's important to share comparison on this dimension between middle eastern and western/northern European nations:

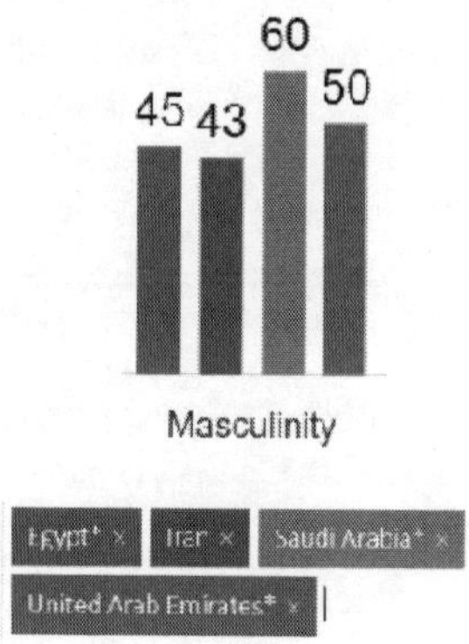

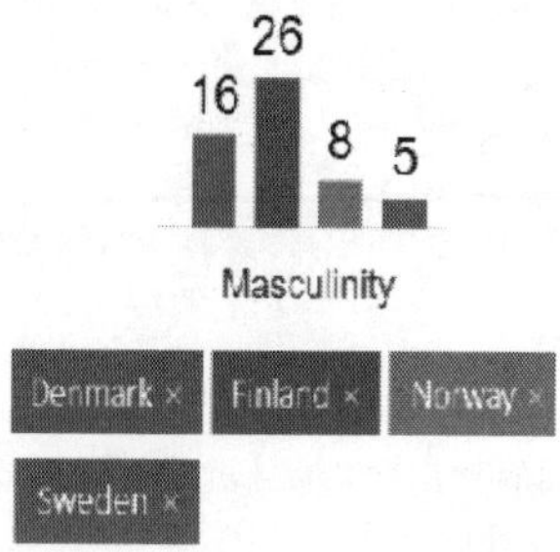

The positioning of masculinity in the complex social interactions nurtured by tourist suppleness and the creation of new and developing tourist spaces finds its due place in many studies done around this subject. Through observing how tourist enactments of masculinity interact and potentially conflict with the gender performances of others, the offers for solo travellers gives us an insight into wider notions of how masculinities are negotiated through relational, performances within tourist spaces and through tourist practice.

The fact that most of the travel's done by my Danish friend Martin, were solo across less explored places, is a testament of the perspectives argued above.

Uncertainty Avoidance Index (Uai)

The Uncertainty Avoidance dimension expresses the degree to which the members of a society feel uncomfortable with uncertainty and ambiguity. Countries exhibiting strong UAI maintain rigid codes of belief and behaviour, and are intolerant of unorthodox behaviour and ideas. Weak UAI societies maintain a more relaxed attitude in which practice counts more than principles.

As presented and argued in paper published in 2020 by Sushant Kumar and Amandeep Dhir, "Associations between travel and tourism competitiveness and culture", the authors while exploring associations between wider variety of cultural studies and travel, have briefly also touched based on the topic of uncertainty avoidance and it's reflection on travel & tourism in a country. According to Kumar and Dhir (2020):

> "Uncertainty-avoiding cultures put efforts into reducing the probability of any situations through the use of stringent behavioral codes of conduct, regulations, guidelines, and condemnation of non-standard beliefs. These efforts are reflected in stringent safety norms that may conflict with individual freedom. The encroachment of a destination's regulations on the freedom of tourists may cause irritation that reduces their preference for popular destinations. On the other hand, countries with lower uncertainty avoidance levels may allow people to experiment since they generally have less stringent rules and policy guidelines. Destinations with relaxed rules tend to be better suited to the purposes of tourists, and their competitiveness is likely to be higher."

My US Born friend, Samantha's reference to uncertainty of Quality & performance in relation to the services offered by Russian

Carrier, is a strong indication of her cultural background and mindset, while she, right from her childhood is programmed to follow set & proven systems, rules and procedures resulting into higher positive & predictable results. To add to this perspective, higher score on Individualism as well, adds to that based on her experiences and perceptions.

Long Term Orientation Versus Short Term Normative Orientation (Lto)

Every society has to maintain some links with its own past while dealing with the challenges of the present and the future. Societies prioritise these two existential goals differently.

Societies who score low on this dimension, for example, prefer to maintain time-honored traditions and norms while viewing societal change with suspicion. Those with a culture which scores high, on the other hand, take a more pragmatic approach: they encourage thrift and efforts in modern education as a way to prepare for the future.

The shift we witness in this space is strongly aligned to understanding of a society and its link with its own roots & history. Countries like India, which is a beautiful melting pot of cultures and societies from civilisations since time immortal to ever more progressing IT & IT services producing world class present a broad spectrum of tourist destinations for all types of travellers. Higher score on this dimension usually presents a notion of challenge like presented in paper by Songshan (Sam) Huang&John C. Crotts, titled "Relationships between Hofstede's cultural dimensions and tourist satisfaction: A cross-country cross-sample examination", where they concluded 'Long Term Orientation are negatively correlated to satisfaction', I intend to think otherwise, which gets backed strongly by "World Economic Forum (WEF)'s ranking of countries best equipped to welcome tourists in 2019". Amongst top 10 tourist friendly countries to visit, Germany & Japan feature as well, while they score very high on this index, while US & Spain too are part of the top block while they score less on this dimension (as compared to other two)

I believe, the mere generalisation of likeliness for a country to support Transnational & Global Forms of Cultural Exchange would not be fair, until it's put through other perspectives linked to dynamic economic setup, political & sociological setup, gender parity and interests that drive cross border tourism.

Indulgence versus Restraint (Ivr)

Indulgence stands for a society that allows relatively free gratification of basic and natural human drives related to enjoying life and having fun. Restraint stands for a society that suppresses gratification of needs and regulates it by means of strict social norms.

Since this dimension, somehow directly relate to our tendency to relax and explore, I would like to take straight dip into the clear contrast we see between Sumeeth (being from India) and my other three friends Martin from Denmark, Samantha from US and Eveline from South Africa.

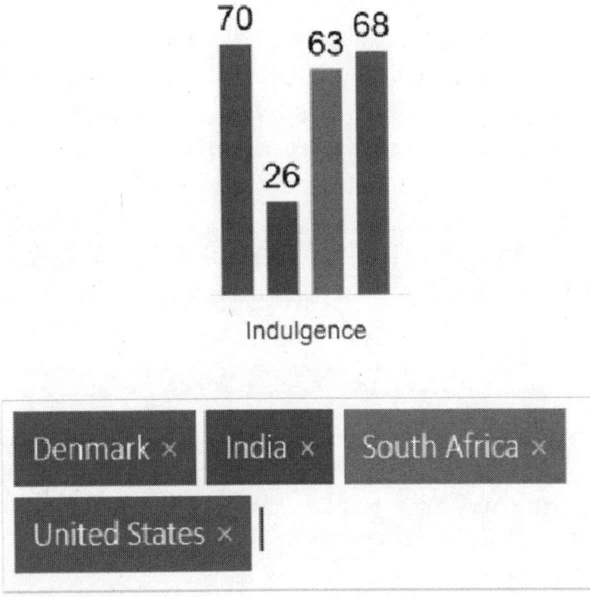

Reflecting upon the graph we as Indians seem to be less indulgent on this idea of enjoying life and having fun, which may sound ridiculous to my fellow Indians, but putting it into perspective of International Leisurely travel, it starts making sense to me at least. Although currency and its conversion value would have a huge role to play in it, but how many times do we even plan a travel abroad? … If travelling with family may cost more, will we be ready to go solo on our exploration of a foreign land? … even while on a trip to another country, can we promise to ourselves to not crave for Only Indian food, rather explore local cuisines? … can we truly and completely commit to be 100% indulgent without fear of being judged by our own kinds?...

I'm afraid, the answer to most of these questions would be a close negative, but again the fact that we move with time and are a progressive society would definitely help us see a huge shift, particularly into this dimension.

To conclude from where I started, that day at Sheremetyevo International Airport, Russia, I may have gone through an extra set of security checks due to my ridiculous body language, but those previous three weeks of discussions, studies and introspections helped me build an outlook that is driven by comparative perspectives beautifully outlined by numerous numbers of years of research that has gone to understand and make this world a better place to live in. As Indian these conclusive thoughts would be incomplete without digging deeper into the research perspectives that we can focus on, especially with the mindset of moving forward on the path of being accepted as a preferred destination. Research Models, like Hofstede's, definitely help us build a foundation, which then needs to be scaled up by adding further dimensions in order to build a broader and more inclusive perspective for future.

References

Geert Hofstede, *Gert Jan Hofstede and Michael Minkov, Cultures and Organisations: Software of the Mind.* Revised and expanded 3rd Edition. 550 pages. New York: McGraw-Hill USA, 2010. ISBN 978-0-07-166418-9.

Zhang, Yingsha; Wu, Tong (Stoltzer); and Li, Xiang (Robert), "The Impacts of Cultural Values on Bilateral. International Tourism Flows" (2015). *Travel and Tourism Research Association:* Advancing Tourismhttps://scholarworks.umass.edu/cgi/viewcontent.cgi?article=1117&context=ttra

Shri.P.C.Cyriac, Sh. *Fakhre A*lam. India Tourism Statistics 2019. https://tourism.gov.in/sites/default/files/2020-04/India%20Tourism%20Statistics%202019.pdf

https://www.adrianbruegger.com/post/cultural-differences/

Henrich, J., Heine, S. J., & Norenzayan, A. (2010). *The weirdest people in the world? Behavioral and Brain Sciences,* 33(2-3), 61-83.

https://www.cambridge.org/core/journals/behavioral-and-brain-sciences/article/abs/weirdest-people-in-the-world/BF84F7517D56AFF7B7EB58411A554C17

SushantKumara, Amandeep Dhir, *Associations between travel and tourism competitiveness and culture*, Received 1 March 2020, Revised 27 September 2020, Accepted 5 October 2020, Available online 20 October 2020. Science Direct.

https://www.sciencedirect.com/science/article/pii/S2212571X20301232

Anna Bruce-Lockhart, These are the top countries for travel and tourism in 2019, https://www.weforum.org/agenda/2019/09/most-travel-tourism-competitive-countries-2019/

CHAPTER 8

Mystical Inclinations in Journey: A Study of Tagore's Travel Poems

Dr. Mamta Chanwaria

Abstract

Life is a chronology of natural and spontaneous occurrences. One may plan his movements and destinations from time to time and this makes travel a part of the entire journey of life. Truthful accounts of a traveler's experiences influence the reader and take him to a mental and emotional ride. Words become divine when they transcend these phenomenal experiences making its impact everlasting. Nobel Laureate Rabindranath Tagore wrote spiritual and magical poetry and has relentless longing to express the mystical and the metaphysical element through his creation. In this article I have tried to explore three of his selected travel poems which reflect the poet's prophetic vision, spiritual wistfulness, and ecological wisdom, oneness with nature and mystical inclinations in his poetry and make travel an infinite experience for his reader.

Keywords: Travel, Life, Journey, Experience, Mystical.

> We are travelers on a cosmic journey, stardust, swirling and dancing in eddies and whirlpools of infinity. Life is eternal. We have stopped for a moment to encounter each other, to meet, to love, to share. This is a precious moment. It is a little parenthesis in eternity.
>
> Paulo Coehlo

Life is a constant journey. We come across different people, places, situations, experiences and destinations and we keep moving on. Every soul has an exclusive, distinct journey. We are all on a path unknown and hence it is said that life is a journey not a destination. This eternal journey leads a soul towards self-realisation and liberation.

Danish author Hans Christian Andersen says, 'To travel is to live'. Journey can be physical, emotional, imaginary, real, material or spiritual. Whatever the form, one thing is sure – one never returns as the same person after his journey. Journeys teach the best lessons of life and enrich one with immense experience. A traveler may come across oasis and deserts, flowers and forests it draws him close to nature and establish a harmony between the two. Chinese philosopher Lao Tzu said, a journey of a thousand miles begin with a single step and that a good traveler has no fixed plans – he is not intent at arriving. A pilgrim feels amazed and blessed by his journey and however tiring and stressful his venture may be, it super cedes his peaceful days.

Man is a wanderer and the impulse to travel is natural to him. All those who have shared their experiences and record of journey through their writings have helped the readers enhance their understanding. A reader follows the path of traveler when he undertakes his journey and for an imaginative reader the mind travels even before the steps actually move. Ibn Batuta, the Moroccan scholar and explorer rightly said that travelling leaves you speechless and then turns you to a story teller.

In this article, I have selected three travel poems of the distinguished and eminent writer, Rabindranath Tagore, whose passion for poem and travel speak for itself. A genius, an artist, philosopher an educator, and reformer popularly known as Gurudev was awarded the Nobel Prize for Literature in 1913 for his sensitive and beautiful verse Gitanjali, originally composed in Bangla and translated to English with consummate skill which became a part of literature of the west because of his fine expression. Exploring and analysing poems of such a literary repute is a wonderful experience in itself.. These poems are, *'I Travelled the Old Road', The Journey'* and *'Journey Home'*. Tagore's poetic thought and expression on journey is enticing and alluring. His vision and his experience is well expressed through his poetic thought and this piece of writing is a humble effort to probe into, to move with and to procure the different shades and aspects of journey through his colloquial and natural verses.

I Travelled the Old Road

This poem is like a breath of fresh air, a journey back to childhood and innocence. It underlies the yearning of freedom and natural life in all of us. Travel is the only experience which retains our innocence, otherwise the more experienced we become the more we lose our innocence. In this sense it is a poem of reliving and celebrating child hood and its goodness.

A very simple and spontaneous expression written in five stanzas the poem takes us to a world of nature and eternal ambience.

'I travelled the old road every day; I took my fruits to the market …..'

At the outset, the poet portrays a picture of the daily activities and responsibilities of the traveler where the routine as well as the route both are very familiar to him. As usual he carries his basket of fruits to the market travelling through a road which he says is 'old' – a familiar one, he took his cattle to the meadows, also ferried his boat across the stream, as it was his daily responsibility and therefore all the ways, the path, the surroundings, everything was well known to him. Nothing was new to the traveler and hence nothing was exciting or pleasant.

'All the ways were well known to me'

The closing line of the first stanza is meaningful and it expresses the monotony of a routine life.

'One morning my basket was heavy with wares'

The second stanza is the extension of the mundane tedious humdrum of human life. The traveler says that men were busy in fields, the cattle in the pastures and the ripening crop all formed a daily dull atmosphere around him.

'Suddenly there was a tremor in the air ….'

Here the traveler undergoes a mesmerising effect – he feels a quivering in the air and the sky seemed very near to him opening new vistas of natural beauty and aura around him. He felt as if he is in a new world and the haze has all cleared around him.

'My mind started up like the morning out of mist'

Here morning symbolizes a fresh new experience, where the daily monotonous route is left behind and a new path and novel surroundings emerge.

'I forgot to follow the track …….'

The traveler admits that he has forgotten his way which means he feels himself lost. Though he takes a few more steps ahead but everything seems strange to him now.

'……..and my familiar world appeared strange to me…..'

The daily track and the daily activities are all left behind and a new track – track towards childhood and freedom is manifest

The concluding stanza is the essence of the poem and of the poet's vision about journey.

> 'My everyday wisdom was ashamed ......'

The traveler sheds all material wisdom as it is futile when one realise the drift and gist of eternal childhood – a state of freedom, innocence, and bliss.

> 'It was the best luck of my life that I lost my path that morning and found my eternal childhood'.

The traveler considers it to be his best luck that he lost his path – the old path which he took every day which was familiar to him, he is now happy and content to lose that path as he has found a new one which has returned him his childhood. Travel is the way to be lost and found at the same time. The poet is astray in a fairyland.

The poem '*I Traveled the Old Road*' is a journey from adulthood to childhood; from toiling to rest; from monotony to excitement; from wisdom to innocence – a simple, touching and enchanting verse by a marvelous poet.

The Journey

'*The Journey*' adheres thematically to eternity and divinity. Here the 'Journey' is an extended metaphor for the spiritual attainment. The ultimate power 'the Almighty' is in the nature around us and this realisation brings one close to His glory. This poem deliberates the presence of Divine in the material manifestations and also establishes that among a group of travelers everyone's experience on the same path is entirely different.

The first movement marks the onset of a journey in which the poet along with his companions move with fast pace without noticing any of their surroundings. There are birds singing around, beautiful flowers dancing merrily and the golden hue through the clouds but they were in such a hurry that they did not notice any of these aesthetics and moved on hastily.

The morning sea of silence broke into ripples of bird songs.....

> ....While we busily went on our way and paid no heed'

The poet admits that they all ignored the beautiful morning scene which is the expression of the glory and beauty of Divine. 'The morning sea of silence' is an exquisite metaphor – the silence is vast and deep as a sea. This ignorance towards the natural beauty indicates that we have so much peace, beauty and happiness around us but we are not aware of this immense treasure. We are on the path of material journey neglecting the myriad nature and divinity around.

> 'We sang no glad songs nor played
> ....We spoke not a word nor smiled
> We lingered not on the way ......'

In the second movement the poet says that he along with his companions moved on their way in such a manner that they did not even enjoy their journey. Neither did they sing nor played which depicts that they were so serious and somber on the way that they did not wish to sing in happiness or to play in a light mood. They did not go to the village to accomplish their daily activities and requirements. They did not even speak to each other and even forgot to smile.

This shows that man is so busy in his material objects that he is simply indifferent to the natural joys and enormous beauty on his way. Hence, he is hastily moving ahead and do not stop to realise or adore the wonderful world of eternal beauty.

The third movement is a turning point in the journey as the poet notices that with the noon time and the sun in the mid sky the humans as well as the birds and flowers all come to a relaxing mode. He says that the doves cooed in the shade, the withered leaves whirled and even a shepherd became drowsy and lay down under a banyan tree.

> 'And I laid myself down by the water
> And stretched my tired limbs on the grass'

The impression and emanation persuade the poet to lie down and take some rest and he stretches his tired limbs on the grass by the water. This expresses the poet's desire to tune up with the nature, to relax for some time, to see and enjoy the immense beauty spreading all over and toinhale the sweet fragrance and immerse himself in the magical surroundings.

> 'My companions laughed at me in scorn;
> They held their heads high and hurried on;

The fourth movement portrays the reaction of the poet's companions who laughed at him scornfully when he decided to take some rest. They kept moving on in disdain and neither did they look back nor did they take any rest and the poet could see them vanishing in the far away mist. Here the poet is separated with his companions on their journey and the poet is now on a different place and his companions on the same path ahead. This shows that even on a common path different travelers have different experiences and perceptions.

The fifth movement is about the poet's companions' progress of their journey. They cross many pastures, hills, unknown lands and countries. The poet shows his appreciation and honor to his companions for their incessant journey. At the same time he feels disturbed and hurt by the mockery and rebuke of his companions and this stimulates him to rise and try to accompany them but he could not rise because his inner self did not respond to do so.

'Mockery and reproach pricked me to rise
But found no response in me'.

This deviate the path of the poet from the path of his companions and he listens to his inner voice and urge and his journey takes a new turn with this call.

'I gave myself up for lost
In the depth of a glad humiliation
.... in the shadow of a dim delight'.

The sixth movement expresses the mental and emotional frame of the poet. A paradoxical ambiguity is spreading all over. The traveler is lost and he says he has accepted his situation. He is no more affected by the mockery of his companions. A new vista has opened. The traveler is delighted – the dim delight is the spark within, the light of the soul which leads to self – realisation and to the happiness and beauty around.

'The repose of the sun-embroidered green gloom
Slowly spread over my heart'.

The poet in this seventh movement feels that the stillness of the dim light of sun spreads over his heart and he has by now forgotten the purpose of his journey and he surrendered himself and all his thoughts without any conflict to the bewildering shadows and songs that natural beauty offered on his way.

The concluding movement is the ultimate achievement of the poet's journey – the eternity and divinity.

'At last when I woke from my slumber and opened my eyes,
I saw thee standing by me, flooding my sleep with smile'

This is the blissful state of the poet's journey. At last when the poet awakes from his sleep and envisions the Almighty blessing him with his smile he realises that his journey has now been accomplished. Also, he accepts that he was apprehensive of the long and tiring path and that reaching to this destination would be so struggle some and hard. The inner voice and the inner light is the way to happiness and taking a breath to feel and admire the natural beauty and eternity is the real path to the glory of God.

> 'How I had feared that the path was long and wearisome,
> And the struggle to reach thee was hard!

Illuminating and inspiring, this poem makes us travel the inner and outer realms along with the traveler. In fact this idea of travel is a fine expression of Tagore's creativity and his philosophy.

Journey Home

Tagore himself was a keen traveler. He often wrote about his travelling experiences. One can notice both simple submission as well as mystical inclinations in his works. *'Journey Home'* describes the poet's travel until he reaches the inner most destination of self-consciousness. It is written in blank verse and has no rhyme scheme. It marks the writer's belief of the presence of sacred godhead within us all and the journey is in fact a discovery of this essence within.

Journey is a metaphor for life and its experiences, the wilderness, the troubles and the efforts to accomplish it. In the very first line the traveler says that the time and the way of journey both have been very long.

> '.........pursued my voyage in the wilderness of worlds
> Leaving my track on many a star and planet.'

The poet says that the inception of his journey has been very natural; it started on a chariot with the first sparkle of light. He passed through the deserts, forests and wastelands which is symbolic of the different experiences of life and left behind his path on many a star and planet.

The most far away course comes closer to the traveler. And life's simplest lessons are learnt through the toughest of experiences. As the poet says,

> 'And that training is the most intricate which leads to the utter simplicity of a tune'.

The journey of life makes a person go to many foreign places, people and situations and then only one realises that his journey concludes with the search and travel within. In fact it is the poet's vision of life – he associates life with journey and all wanderings with experience, inner quest and the ultimate realisation.

> 'and one has to wander through all the outer
> worlds to reach the innermost shrine at the end'.

The traveler wandered a lot before he could actually realise he has reached his destination. All his turbulence comes to an end with the assurance of his consciousness. As Tagore has concluded'

> 'The question and the cry 'Oh, Where?' melt into tears of a thousand
> Streams and deluge the world with the flood of the assurance 'I am'!

All the confusion has come to an end and only remains is the assurance of self. There is a lot of wandering before reaching; a lot of toiling before reaping, lot of intricacies before simplicity and the long and time consuming journey ultimately takes the traveler to his innermost altar!

Tagore's persistent longing to express the mystical and metaphysical is evident in his writings especially when it comes to poem and more specifically when it comes to travel poems. Words express thought in the simplest of form but they become divine when it radiates the spiritual yearning and prophetic vision of the master. Travel is all about exploration and experience. Life is a series of natural and spontaneous occurrences and we all are travelers on an unknown path. One should let it flow in a natural course and enjoy and admire the beauty and serenity around as well as within! Every traveler has his own perception, vision, passion and also the liberty to pause, to divert, to deluge, to meditate, to be one with nature and meet oneself. As famous American poet, Robert Frost has also expressed in his poem 'The Road Not Taken':

> 'Two roads diverged in a wood, and I-
> I took the one less travelled by,
> And that has made all the difference'.

The poems I analysed in this article are simple yet captivating and the reader travels along with the thoughts of the poet travelling within and without. A traveler remembers what he has seen but at the same time he sees and experiences more than he remembers. Yes, everyone is on his distinct journey – journey guided by the inner spirit.

References

https// tripinfi.com

https// www.indianeagle.com

https//www.poemhunter.com

https//owlcation.com

https//www.livehistoryindia.com

https//allpoetry.com

https//famouspoetsandpoems.com

CHAPTER 9

A Kaleidoscopic view of Paul Theroux's *The Great Railway Bazaar*

Dr. Rashmi Bhatnagar

Abstract

Paul Theroux an American novelist's, *The Great Railway* Bazaar, published in 1975 is an entertaining and exhaustive railway Odyssey undertaken in 1973. It's a grand journey beginning from Europe in the Direct Orient Express which links Europe to Asia. The journey to many destinations is undertaken by Khyber pass local, the Frontier mail, The Golden Arrow to Kuala Lumpur, the Mandal Express and the Trans-Siberian express.

Keywords: Journey, Destination, Express, Railway

Travel like a train
Narrow
Straight
Undisturbed, destined....

Theroux admits that he developed the fascination for trains from his early childhood. He writes," Those whistles sing bewitchment: Railways are irresistible bazaars, making a long perfectly level no matter what the landscape improving your mood with speed and never upsetting your drink. (TGRB, 1).

What is remarkable about the book is that it is written like a travel narrative, truly reflecting on what the author observes during the course of his journey. It is at the same time contrived like a novel. While history books can deliver to us facts about people and events of times past, traveloguesdescribe the sounds, sights and smells that give those facts context." (http://thelittlemanreviews.wordpress.com)

Theroux writes in his book, "All travel circular. I have been jerked through Asia, making a parabola on one of the planets hemispheres. After all, the Grand Tour is just the inspired man's way of heading home." He also writes," The difference between the travel writing and fiction is the difference between recording what the eye sees and discovering what the imagination knows. Fiction is pure joy how sad that I could not reinvent the trip as fiction." (TGRB, 354)

The book portrays not only the outer atmosphere, scenes and pictures but also the interactive episodes of fascinated men he meets in the journey. What catches the Reader's attention is," The singularity of what isfleeting: Visual Impressions and talk". (http://www.kirbusreview.com). The writer himself admits that what he was looking for and what he found. The line in the text," I sought trains: I found passengers" sums it all. The writer thoroughly enjoys the journey and the book is more of a personal account of the journey rather than something else. Each train that he boards offers new emotions, characters and interactions. We feel fresh and different with each change of train and place.

Theroux beautifully writes," Anything is possible on a train: A great meal, a binge, a visit from card players, intrigue, a good night sleep, and stranger's monologues framed like Russian short stories." (TGRB,)

Each train journey in individual chapters is a route with stops and delays intermixed. It is a journey in 32 chapters and nearly 500 pages. Each chapter is a medley of local colours, encounters with varied people, different situations and many small things which are observed but go unnoticed. He quotes extensively from other writers and their views. Theroux is not only interested in the world outside the window but also in the life inside the compartments. His characters leave an indelible impression on the reader's mind. Sadiq – the buggy, whom he meets on the Tehran express, does not cast a favourable impression on him. Theroux writes, "Sadik smiled; he had crooked teeth. It is not skinny people who look hungry, but rather fat ones, and Sadik looked famished." Mr Bhardwaj – the prime ascetic Indian accountant, carrying on external losing campaign against lighters and his office in India – the drunk man and Mr Chatterjee whom he meets on the train are people who cast an impression on him, during the course of his journey.

In another encounter on the Kalka mail to Shimla, he writes about Bengalis whom he interacts with. "The Kalka mail was full of Bengalis, on their way to Shimla for a festival, the Kali puja. Bengalis, whose complexion resembles that of black goddess of destruction they worship..." The many characters whom he meets in the journey give him different insights of life. Theroux visits many places and meets many people and he comes to this conclusion that, " the conversation, like many others I had with people on trains, derived an easy candour from the shared journey, the comfort of the dining car, and the certain knowledge that neither of us would see each other again. The railway was a fiction's bazaar, in which anyone with the patience could carry away a memory to pore over in privacy. (TGRB, 71)

Theroux's characters come to life as we move from Europe, the Middle East, India, Southeast Asia and Japan before returning back by trans-Siberian Railway. The essence of each Nation is put forward through the journey by different trains. He writes," The trains in any country contain the essential paraphernalia of the culture. Thai trains have the Shower jar with the gloves Dragon on its sides...... Indian ones a vegetarian kitchen and 6 classes, Iranian one's prayer mats, Malaysian one's a noodle stall, Vietnamese one's bulletproof glasses on the locomotive, and on every character of a Russian train there is a samovar". Places and platforms are also described with a critic's eye. Few trains have special mention, like the Turkish railways of which Theroux writes, "I was reassured of what I saw of Turkish railways: the train was long and solid, the sleeping car was newer than the wagon-lit on the direct-orient, the dining car had fresh flowers on the tables and was well stocked with wine and beer." (TGRB, 47) similarly he writes about Khyber railways, "Built fifty years ago at a great cost, it is an engineering marvel. It has thirty-four tunnels, ninety-two bridges and culverts, and climbs to 3600 feet. The Khyber rifles stand sentry duty…" (TGRB, 75)

His Style of presenting things is witty and peppered with observations. " I looked out of the window and saw the strangest sight – children, girls and boys of anywhere from seven to twelve, the younger ones naked, the older ones wearing loincloths, were leaping off the train carrying cans of water. They were wild children, with long lank hair faded brown by the sun, with black shoulders and dusty faces and snub noses – like Australian aborigines-.." (TGRB, 152)

The book has snapshots of almost everything. It includes sketches of countries, the railway stations, the interior of the trains, the outer landscape and most important. The capture of characters. Each character, scene, description is lively and captivating. Paul theroux had always loved trains, ever since he was a little boy. "Hearing them pierce the night outside his Massachusetts home as a boy". (TGRB, 1) Trains are not just a pleasant mode of travel and entertainment, but are also a microcosm of society. Just as he finishes the physical travel from one corner of the world to another, in the same manner he pens off "Ever since childhood, when I lived within earshot of the Boston and Maine, I have seldom heard a train go by and not wished I was on it."(TGRB, 355)

The book offers a delightful reading, especially in today's time where travelling is reduced to minimum. Long journeys have been simplified by air travel. Having time and inclination to undertake a long journey like Theorux is simply unimaginable. Just as one sits near a window, in a train journey and watches the outside and the inside, in the same manner Theroux's book takes us everywhere.

References

Theroux, Paul. *The Great Railway Bazaar.* Penguin Books, 1975.

https://www.nytimes.com

https://www.kirbusreviews.com

https://thelittlemanreviews.wordpress.com

CHAPTER 10

Journeying with Frost through Life

Dr. Atiqa Kelsy

Abstract

Robert Frost is not only known for using symbols to express the practical wisdom of a farmer but also elevating that local wisdom to the universal level. Among those symbols, traveling or journeying form an important part of Frost's oeuvre. For the present study, some of Frost's poems that use travel, journey as a constant symbol of life that goes in and as it goes on, people learn, people grow and pick up lessons on the way as they go ahead in their journey of life.

Keywords: Journey, Symbol, Life, spiritual, Poems.

Symbols have been indefinitely used in human interaction and communication to express complex feelings and emotions. Symbols not only lend charm to our expression but also are sometimes the best medium to convey the otherwise inexpressible. One such timeless symbol that has been used across eras and cultures is the symbol of a journey or travel. This could be because of our nomadic origins, our desire to explore beyond the known realms, our sense of adventures and also our need to have some fulfillment in terms of accomplishments. Robert Frost is not only known for using symbols to express the practical wisdom of a farmer but also elevating that local wisdom to the universal level. Among those symbols, traveling or journeying forms an important part of Frost's oeuvre. For the present study, some of Frost's poems that use travel, journey as a constant symbol of life that goes in and as it goes on, people learn, people grow and pick up lessons on the way as they go ahead in their journey of life.

In fact, one feels that Frost was preoccupied with using the universal symbol of travel as the journey of life with its challenge, dilemma, obstacles, promises and mystery. '*Two Roads Diverged in a Wood*' reflects the poet upon facing confusing choices in the journey of life. The poet realises he cannot have both the worlds and he will have to make a choice which makes him sad. The entire poem titled '*The Road Not Taken*' is like the poet's mind under the reader's microscope who is examining the process of how the poet comes to the conclusion of traveling "the one less travelled by". On reading deeper one also feels a sense of regret or a sense of loss, a mystery that remains unknown to the poet till the end, because he would never know what life would have been if he had taken the other road. At the beginning of the poem, the poet despairs at the fact that being a single traveller he "could not travel both". Realising that it is a lifelong choice, the poet does stare long and hard, takes his time to think before deciding. But not matter what; making one choice will always leave unanswered questions for '*The Road Not Taken*', the reason why the poem is also not titled otherwise, The Road Taken! The poem concludes on an ambivalent note. The poet imagines recalling this very decision with a sigh at a later stage in his life, perhaps old age, narrating his life story to his grandchildren or old acquaintances! There is a travelling into the future through this imagined telling and then a travel in the past through the looking glass of memory, concluding that he took the "one less travelled by, and that has made all the difference." The ambivalence referred to above lingers, like the sigh, in the concluding lines – is the difference good or is it not as wonderful as the writer might have imagined or wanted to! The poet never makes it clear and we shall never know, just as the poet did not at the time of making the choice, just as we never know when we make such a choice in our lives. The sigh and the difference remain for time to tell, plus the other road's mystery never lets us settle with a definitive answer. The road that one gives up on to travel the road of choice never leaves us in peace. We always wonder with Ifs and Buts!!! The conclusion reminds one of a longer and more philosophical poem of Frost, titled '*West-Running Brook*'. The poem might have been inspired by a passage in Henri Bergson's book '*Creative Evolution*' (1911), which Frost had read and was greatly influenced by:

> Life as a whole, from the initial impulsion that thrust it into the world, will appear as a wave which rises, and which is opposed by the descending movement of matter.... this rising wave is consciousness.... [Individual souls] are nothing else than the little rills into which the great river of life divides itself, flowing through the body of humanity.' (Creative Evolution, 269-70.)

'The West-Running Brook' also talks about life as a journey as represented by the brook. But it is a west running brook when all the brooks run east. The lines echo a similar sentiment of travelling the road less travelled by, going against convention, breaking the norm, doing things contrary to the general way and living life unconventionally:

> the brook runs west.'
> 'West-running Brook then call it.'
> (West-Running Brook men call it to this day.)
> 'What does it think it's doing running west
> When all the other country brooks flow east
> To reach the ocean? It must be the brook
> Can trust itself to go by contraries

The brook is bold enough to trust itself with contraries, similar to the poet. What inspires the poet to take the road less travelled by also remains equally unknown just as the brook's reason to run west is not mentioned in the poem. Emerson, another poet whom Frost admired greatly uses a similar metaphor of a stream to talk about the enigma that humankind is in his essay *'The Over-Soul'*, where he writes, "Man is a stream whose source is hidden."

'Stopping by the Woods on a Snowy Evening' is another poem that uses journey as symbol of the mesmerising mystery of life. The poet stops "between the woods and frozen lake" on his way back home, a wandering soul on this planet earth. His horse too finds it strange as he stops "without a farmhouse near" on what he calls "the darkest evening of the year". The darkest evening, the woods and the snow slowly filling it up can all be used to symbolise different aspects of life. The darkest evening represents those moments in life when life seems bleak, discouraging and tiring, while snow refers to the obstacles of life that make our journey more challenging, the woods is the symbols of life itself where the pilgrims are sent for a particular period of time before they head back to their original home – heaven. The owner of the woods could be seen as a divine figure, God or a supernatural power that is omniscient. The poem ends with the most famous lines in literature clearly emphasising the symbolic vitality underneath the deceptively simple façade created by the poem. The poem thus is Frost's masterpiece as he adeptly manages to describe his journey back to his village after a day's work in town as a deep allegory for life itself.

'*Birches*' can be considered as an unusual poem depicting vertical travel, an attempt to reach heaven and the descent back as the speaker in the poem realises that "Earth's the right place to love: I don't know where it's likely to get better." The boy that the speaker imagines not only travels upwards on every Birch tree till he subdues them but also horizontally from one Birch to another. The travel in this poem gets mystical as it proceeds from simple imaginative boy that the poet prefers to think is responsible for bending the Birches. His adult logic does tell him it is the storm that bends the Birches but he still prefers to imagine that a boy like him swings on the branches day in and day out, all day till they bend surrendering to incessant swinging. The reader immediately wonders why the poet wishes to imagine a boy swinging on the branches of the trees and bending them. The answer comes towards the end, where Frost confesses that he himself was once "a swinger of birches." Thus, we get to know at this point that this poem is not merely about horizontal and vertical travel but also a journey into the poet's past! Every time the poet sees bent birches, the poet's mind travels back in time, Proustian style, searching for lost time. The poem reads like an allegory of life from these lines onwards. Frost longs to go back to being a swinger of birches because he feels whenever "life is too much of a pathless wood where your face burns and tickles with the cobwebs broken across it, and one eye is weeping from a twig's having lashed across it open." That is the time when he would prefer to "get away from earth awhile". The poet makes it clear though that this is not an escape. He is very much a man of this ground, this earth – he states, "Earth's the right place for love: I don't know where it's likely to get better." He only wants to get away upwards for a while, maybe to have a better view of earthly things from a little distance up above, to also renew his waning strength or maybe just momentarily escape and come back to life with renewed vigour! Life's journey needs to be escaped vertically sometimes to be able to live better and fuller. He therefore makes it clear to treacherous fate, not to "willfully misunderstand" him and "half grant" his wish by snatching him away in the middle of life happening so that he is never able to return. All he wants to do is:

> ...climbing a birch tree,
> And climb black branches up a snow-white trunk
> Toward *heaven*, till the tree could bear no more,
> But dipped its top and set me down again.
> That would be good both going and coming back.

> One could do worse than be a swinger of birches.

The word 'heaven' has been italicized to probably make the reader pay more attention to the possible reference to heaven as some divine authority's dwelling place or the vertical travel that the poet desires to undertake.

Another poem that uses the analogy of journey or travel is a long and more philosophical poem of Frost that looks at life not only as a journey but also as a quest. The person walking on the road of life is on a quest where the traveller is seeking for

> a house that is no more a house
> Upon a farm that is no more a farm
> And in a town that is no more a town.

The road leading to this place is also as ambiguous as the place.

> The road there, if you'll let a guide direct you
> Who only has at heart your getting lost

The poem is not only a quest of an individual but also a quest for humanity at large with the monoliths, wagon with iron wheels, glaciers, and quarry. The poem is also about the poet's spiritual journey, "And there's a story in a book about it:" and reference to the number 40, the sign saying CLOSED, and reference to the brook, the grail, St Mark and the goblet. The poet again insists in the second half of the poem once again that the only way to find oneself is to lose oneself, "And if you're lost enough to find yourself by now". In the end, Frost shows the reader what he had been led to:

> Here are your waters and your watering place.
> Drink and be whole again beyond confusion.

As the poem proceeds, one realises that the poem is about Frost's spiritual quest for finding a resting place for his Faith that puts this strange restlessness, this feeling of being lost and never found or the spiritual uncertainty that Frost is going through at this point in his life. The poem is written in his seventies that explains the meditative mood and ambiguous imagery of the poem. The poet is looking back at his life, taking retreating steps back into his past through his youth down to his childhood and finds certain answers. It is a journey within and backwards for the poet and the reader along with him to find answers to his search. The poet finds them not in any creed or any complex religious philosophy or theology.

As Frost journey's back into his childhood, we realise that "the house that once was a house" could be his own childhood home that now remains alive only in his memory. He makes it a little clear. "This was no playhouse but a house in earnest". The poet then realises:

> Your destination and your destiny's
> A brook that was the water of the house

In the Biblical context, water symbolises the Word of God and Jesus Himself. Thus by the end of the journey, Frost resigns to his original childlike Faith in God to reconcile to the truths of life. Jesus was in conversation with the Samaritan Woman and that is when he had said, "but whoever drinks of the water that I will give him shall never thirst; but the water that I will give him will become in him a well of water springing up to eternal life." (The Bible. NIV. John4:14)

The Samaritan woman had come to Jacob's well to draw water where Jesus was sitting, and he had asked her for water. In the ensuing conversation Jesus makes this revelation to the woman. The language that Frost employs is reminiscent of these words of Jesus. Besides the language is the imagery of "A broken drinking goblet like the Grail" that clearly hints at the religious undertone of the poem. He further adds,

> Under a spell so the wrong ones can't find it,
> So can't get saved, as Saint Mark says they mustn't.

The reference is to Mark 4:12, so that, "they may be ever seeing but never perceiving, and ever hearing but never understanding; otherwise, they might turn and be forgiven!" According to the Gospel of Mark, Jesus talked in parables so that only those who understood would be saved. His goblet has a spell so that only the right ones can find it. Finally, he reaches the spring of water and realises all he needs to do is drink from it and be found while he was getting lost all along his life.

Frost finally reconciles with his childhood and childlike faith.

> The road there, if you'll let a guide direct you
> Who only has at heart your getting lost

Is the road that leads to self-discovery? But this self-discovery cannot take place without getting lost on the way. Frost finally gets his spiritual 'Directive' while travelling back into his childhood and retracing his childlike faith. Jesus says in Luke 18:17, "Truly, I say to you, whoever does not receive the kingdom of God like a child shall not enter it." Frost's spiritual quest encourages him to get lost on the way and finally leads him to the well of faith that watered his childhood. The quest is not the quest of Frost alone; it also is the quest of entire humankind!

Thus, we see journey has been an important motif in Frost's poems as he reflects on life, the choices we make, the stopovers we choose, and the destinations we reach. But most importantly the lessons we learn in the quest of life. To conclude in the words of Frost, "In three words I can sum up everything about life: it goes on."

References

Spacey, Andrew. "Analysis of Poem 'West-Running Brook' by Robert Frost". Owlcation. 3 Oct. 2021. 1 Dec. 2021. Web. https://owlcation.com/humanities/Analysis-of-Poem-West-Running-Brook-by-Robert-Frost

Emerson, Ralph Waldo. "Emerson--Essays--The Over-Soul". 09Dec. 2021. Web. <https://archive.vcu.edu/english/engweb/transcendentalism/authors/emerson/essays/oversoul.html>

Rodenhizer, Samuel. "Quotation Celebration". 27 Oct. 2017.09 Dec. 2021. Web. <https://quotationcelebration.wordpress.com/2017/10/27/in-three-words-i-can-sum-up-everything-about-life-it-goes-on-robert-frost/>

CHAPTER 11

Travel Globally with an Open Mind and Heart

Mrs. Anita John

Abstract

Travel has a host of benefits. The restraints of a word limit and the indescribable nature of some of these experiences present a challenging task for anyone who is attempting to pen them down in a few pages. Nonetheless, this article endeavours to bring forth the myriad ways in which travel changes and expands our repertoire of social, emotional and physical well-being. While doing so, it draws upon the author's personal experiences, weaving travel vignettes with the profound life lessons acquired during her travels. These include but are not limited to travel being a stress buster, an important means in expanding your creativity, resilience, empathy, inclusivity perspective and in redefining the very core of your existence. The above listed benefits of travel are also corroborated by empirical research evidence.

Keywords: Travel, Global, Effects, Happiness, self-discovery, resilient, stress buster.

As per an article published in June 2019as a part of the Annual meeting of the new champions, 'curiosity and globalisation are driving a new approach to travel'. The younger generation is now interested in collecting experiences rather than material possessions.

Globalisation is the process of international integration arising from the interchange of views, ideas, product and other aspect of culture. Advances in transportation and telecommunications infrastructure, including the rise of the telegraph and its posterity the Internet, are major factors in globalisation, generating further interdependence of economic and cultural activities.

Positive Effects of Globalisation

Globalisation has played a positive role in changing the lives of millions of people around the world. In the following pointers, we will try to gain an insight into the positive effects of globalisation.

1. Increased Competition between nations pertaining the services and commitments they offer to people who visit them.
2. Earning foreign trade and capital flows through travellers.
3. Spread of technical know-how, customs, traditions, languages with the people who travel that country.

People who travel will probably agree: experiences travelling global change your mindset... for the better. Travel has the power of making us a better human being both socially and mentally. When I think about the benefits of traveling the world as it relates to open-mindedness, I think of all the places I have travelled and life experiences I got from each travel. It's no news that travel is good for your physical wellbeing, but a significant amount of scientific research suggests that exploring a new place can do wonders for your mental and emotional health as well.

A paper published by Elizabeth O' Brien in 2014 studies that travel can boost cognitive and cardiovascular health. Travel tops many people's retirement goals, and it's a given that staying healthy prolongs our ability to take active vacations. Yet research suggests that the reverse holds true as well: Travel can actually keep our brains and bodies healthier as we get older. Travel has been found to lower the risk of heart attack and death from coronary disease in certain groups, while the new and complex situations encountered while traveling can also help keep the brain sharp.

While travelling you undergo a transformation of your mind and heart.

Traveling makes your mind happy and healthy:

1. Travelling is a stress buster

I have had history of neuro strokes due to stress. Travelling has been a real stress buster for me as when I travel; I leave behind all worries of home and work and just relax. "The stress of work and daily demands can distract us from what we find to be actually meaningful and interesting," says Dr. Tamara McClintock Greenberg, a San Francisco-based clinical psychologist and author of '*Psychodynamic Perspectives on Aging and Illness*'. Thus, taking a break from the daily hustle and bustle is essential for your mind to relax, recharge and rejuvenate. When you travel you feel lighter, younger, healthier and surely happier. Traveling promotes happiness and helps you take your mind off stressful situations. This leads to lower cholesterol levels, making you feel calmer and content. "It also helps us reflect on our personal goals and interests," adds Greenberg. According to a 2013 study, more than 80% of Americans, who were surveyed, noticed significant drops in stress just after a day or two of traveling. Travel globally to remove stress from your life.

2. Travelling helps you rediscover yourself

In 2012 when I went to West midland in U.K for a church exchange I rediscovered the rich value systems in India. It was a Sunday morning and I with my other counterparts in the exchange program had to give a presentation with the youth. After the presentation I saw a girl of 12 years playing with a small cute child outside the church. When I asked her whether the child was a younger sibling, she responded giggling that she was the mother of the child. This incident gave me a cultural shock but at the same time I thanked Lord for giving me birth in India where I had not seen a 12-year-old mother. I rediscovered my identity of being a proud Indian. Writer Patrick Rothfuss said, "A long stretch of road can teach you more about yourself than a hundred years of quiet. " Experiential traveling, particularly to a foreign country, can help you re-evaluate and reinvent your life. "If you allow it, travel has the ability to expand your mind in a way you never realised was possible," says solo travel expert and founder of the Trusted Travel Girl, Valerie Wilson. When we don't travel, we take all things available in our country as granted. It is only when we travel, we start valuing our own culture, traditions and your own personality.

3. Travelling Builds Contentment and Happiness

The very thought of travel gives us happiness. The new events and experiences help rewire your brain, hence boosting your mood and self-confidence. Exploring new places can also give you a fresh start if you're recovering from a major loss in your life. After my father passing away nothing could give me comfort more than an outing. According to a Cornell University study, the anticipation of a trip can increase your happiness substantially, even more than the anticipation of acquiring something tangible, like a new car.

4. Travelling makes you more Resilient

Going and living somewhere where you feel excited and intimidated at the same time can help you toughen up mentally and emotionally.

In Coventry one early morning I was informed by my host that Mr O.T Aden who was a dear member in the trip had a cardiac arrest previous night. I was completely shattered by this news as the previous day he was with me helping out carry my shopping bags. Also, facing difficulties in an unfamiliar environment, among new people, forces you to learn and adapt to a life that's out of your comfort zone. This makes you more flexible, patient and emotionally strong. Travel has taught me patience, to surrender control to the uncontrollable and effectively problem solving being more resilient. It can also help you deal with "larger issues in life with more grace and patience," adds a travel expert. Bottom line is, the more challenges you're faced with, the better you'll get at overcoming them, eventually becoming more resilient, mentally and emotionally.

5. Travelling Enhances Originality and Creativity

When I travelled to South Korea, I learnt to be more creative in accepting new options like Bread and Butter and fresh apples as my daily diet as my taste buds couldn't take the food there. Travelling also improves your problem-solving skills. According to Adam Galinsky, a professor at Columbia Business School, visiting a foreign place and immersing yourself in their local environment (for instance, attending a 'snake boat' race in southern India or feasting on crispy tarantulas in Cambodia), increases your cognitive flexibility. It consequently gives a boost to your creativity.

6. Travelling makes one Recognise different Qualities in other Cultures-

I was able to pick out notable differences between western culture and my own (Indian) when I travelled that realm. I saw that the European and American people prioritise self-dignity above all else. For them fulfilling material needs and career is important. Back home in India, I often see families and relationships coming first or second to things like self-esteem, career and financial success. In seeing those key differences, you recognise that not only do people in other parts of the world do things differently, but often times they do it better. Regardless, when shown an alternative, people who travel at least question what they've always known and in doing so, they become open to other ways of doing things. We start respecting other cultures when we travel extensively.

7. Travelling forces you to Ty new things and Meet new People

Ask any travel person spending time abroad will encourage you to get outside of your comfort zone and try things that you probably wouldn't have thought to at home. You meet people with different mindset, culture, social upbringing, eating habits. I've tried more new types of food than I can count. I tried a hike along the steep, spiny ridges of a mountain range and I fell in love with the thrill that comes with hiking and running along really difficult peaks. I think many people get stuck in an established social circle at home and easily go years without meeting anyone new or making a great, new lifelong friend. That's a shame no matter how awesome your friends may be. Those tight-knit friendships are great in many ways but oftentimes, when people settle into a comfortable social circle, they're not as open to meeting new people. I've heard interesting perspectives on topics I had not given much thought to prior. I've learned about different travel styles. In other parts of the world, people speak, eat, work and socialize differently. The way they interact with each other is also different. Yes, people who travel to different lands will find that their perspectives change and their minds become more open minded.

8. Traveling makes you Better understand the Plight of newcomers at home

The benefits of traveling the world come home with you. I think when we talk about the pros of traveling, we often think about the period of time spent away from home. When we're talking about how travel makes you more open-minded, those positives apply to your return home. India is generally a very diverse and welcoming country but now that I've been spending time in countries that aren't my own and speaking a language different from my native one, I have such a better understanding of what the immigrant experience is really like. I've struggled while ordering meals, when being asked basic questions, when trying to give directions, etc. If I've been frustrated by those experiences, I can only sympathise with newcomers at home who maybe don't have the option of returning to their homes and who, along with language barriers, also have to adjust to a harsh climate, culture shock and high costs of living.

9. Your Philosophy of Life Changes

You can forget all the ideas you have around your precious personal space, assumptions about other cultures because guess what? That personal bubble of yours is going to be burst. In India family and close friends are always welcome home for meals but in Europe a daughter would also have to inform her parents if she wishes to have a cup of tea with them once moving out of the family. When I was told by a parent of 13-year-old girl that from now onwards she would have to work, baby sitting or cleaning someone's toilet to cater her school fees, my philosophy of life where a parent is considered to take care of her children until they get married, got completely eroded. Changing ideas around personal space is a test on open-mindedness for everyone. Nothing is wrong completely. This perfectly illustrates how ideas around personal space can become redefined out of necessity while abroad. Being open-minded about that will make the process easier. Yes, sometimes I find the culture to be strange. But you know what? It's also pretty useful in making children independent and self-reliant.

Travel is also good medicine when it comes to brain health, said Paul D. Nussbaum, a Pittsburgh-based psychologist who participated in the Global Coalition on Aging report. While studies isolating the impact of travel are few, plenty of research has suggested that there are brain-boosting benefits to social and leisure experiences. One study found that regular participation in activities such as traveling, odd jobs or gardening was associated with a lower risk of subsequent dementia. In my opinion any person who wishes to travel globally must travel with an open mind and heart to embrace the unknown, respect all cultures and opinions. Travelling can give us life lessons.

References

Forbes life – 'Five reasons why travel is good for your mental health' – Noma Nazish

https://www.forbes.com/sites/nomanazish/2018/01/22/five-reasons-why-travel-is-good-for-your-mental-health/amp/

https://www.webmd.com/mental-health/how-travel-affects-mental-health

https://www.hindustantimes.com/fitness/world-heart-day-5-ways-in-which-travel-can-keep-your-heart-healthy/story-rYQOmOxBALRkkKHnH6PoCM_amp.html

CHAPTER 12

Bernier's *Travels in the Mughal Empire*: A Socio-Religious Perspective

Dr. Prerna Maheshwari

Abstract

The accounts of the travellers provide us lot of information about the native people, their culture, customs and social and religious life. Most of the travellers came from vastly different social and cultural environments. Hence they were more attentive to everyday activities and practices.

Francois Bernier was a French physician, political philosopher, traveller and historian who visited India in the 17th Century. He was associated with the Mughal Court as a personal physician of Dara Shikoh and later as a scientist with Danishmand Khan.

Bernier travelled to different parts of the country and wrote accounts based on his observations. His works were published in France in 1670 and translated into English, Dutch, German and Italian. Bernier's book *'Travels in the Mughal Empire'* provides a detailed account and critical insight of the Mughal time India. This book mainly explores the reigns of DaraShikoh and Aurangzeb. This article makes an attempt to make an assessment of Francois Bernier's travel account in relation to its cultural relevance. An attempt shall be made to present a true picture of Bernier's contribution in analysing Indian social and religious structure under Mughal rule.

Keywords: Beths, Gentiles, Eclipse, Solemnization.

In his letter to Monsieur Chapelain[1], Bernier mentioned the superstitions, strange customs and doctrines of the Hindus.

Vedas

Bernier came to know about the Vedas from Hindus. They told him that God had sent them four books, to which they gave the name of Beths[2], a word signifying science. The four books were named as Atherbabed (Atharvaved), Zagerbed (Yajurved), Rekbed (Regved) andSambed (Samved). These books advocate that the people should be divided into four tribes/casts – first, the tribe of Brahmins, or interpreters of the law; second, the tribe of Quetterys, or warriors; third, the tribe of Bescue, or merchants and tradesmen, commonly called Banyanes; and fourth, the tribe of Seydra, or artisans or labourers. These different tribes were not permitted to intermarry. For instance, a Brahmin could not marry a Quettery.

Bernier illustrated the prevalence of caste system in India by stating as follows, "the embroiderer brings up his son as an embroiderer, the son of a goldsmith becomes a goldsmith and a physician of the city educates his son for a physician. No one marries but in his own trade or profession; and this custom is observed almost as rigidly by Mahametans as by the Gentiles, to whom it is expressly enjoined by their law." (258-260)

The Gentiles (3) believed in a doctrine similar to that of the Pythagoreans with regard to the transmigration of souls, and hold it illegal to kill or eat any animal; an exception being made, however, in favour of the second tribe, provided the flesh eaten be not that of the cow or peacock. For these two species they have a peculiar respect, particularly for the cow, believing that it was by holding to a cow's tail they were to cross the river which separated this life from the next.

The Beths render it obligatory upon every Gentile to say his prayers with his face turned to the East thrice in the twenty four hours: in the morning, at noon, and at night. The whole of his body must also be washed three times or at least before every meal; and he is taught that it is more meritorious to perform his ablutions and to repeat his prayers in running rather than in stagnant water. According to Beths, God created three perfect beings; one was Brahma, a name which signifies penetrating into all things; the second, Beschen/ Vishnu, who, exists in all things; and the third Mehahden, or the mighty lord. By means of Brahma, God created the world; by means of Beschen he upholds it; and by means of Mehahdu he will destroy it. It was Brahma who, by God's command, published the four Beths. The second person in Trinity has been nine times incarnate in consequences of various evils in the world, from which he delivered mankind. Gentiles said that the first incarnation of Beschen was in the form of a Lion, the second in that of a Hog, the third in that of a tortoise, the fourth in that of a serpent, the fifth in that of a dwarfish, only a cubit in height, the sixth was in the form of a monstrous Man-lion, the seventh in that of a Dragon, the eighth as Krishna, the ninth in the nature of an Ape, and the tenth is to be in the person of a mighty Cavalier. The eighth incarnation was the most remarkable forming a major part of Hindu religion over the years

Solar Eclipse

He described the cultural practices followed by Indians during the solar eclipse which he saw from Delhi in 1666. He wrote that at the time fixed for appearance of the eclipse, both shores of the river Jamna (Yamuna) were covered with Idolators, who stood in the water up to the waist, eagerly waiting for the commencement of the eclipse, in order to plunge and wash themselves. The little kids were almost naked; the men had nothing but a scarf round their middle and the married women and girls were covered with a single cloth. He further added that at the beginning of the obscuration of sun, the Idolators plunged their whole body under water several times with a loud cry, then stood in the river, lifted their eyes and hands towards the sun, muttered and prayed with seeming devotion, filling their hands from time to time with water, which they threw in the direction of the sun. He also noted that they threw pieces of silver at a great distance into the Yamuna and gave alms to the Brahmins. Every individual on coming out of the water put on new clothes, placed on the sand for that purpose, and several of the devotees left their old garments as presents for the Brahmins. Bernier wrote a short note on solemnisation of the grand eclipse festival, especially at Thanaiser[3] where more than one hundred and fifty thousand people, assembled from all parts of the empire. On the day of an eclipse, its waters were considered more holy than on other days. He also mentioned that the ceremony was not performed until a certain number of Brahmins had presented the king with a lakh of rupees equal to about fifty thousand crowns; in return he gave them a few vests and an old elephant.

Jagannath Rath Yatra

Another religious practice observed by Bernier was Jagannath Rath Yatra. He gave a detailed account of the place and the festival for which more than one hundred and fifty thousand people were gathered in the town. It was situated on the Gulf of Bengal. The festival continued for eight or nine days. A huge wooden machine was constructed and sat on fourteen or sixteen wheels and pushed by the united exertions of fifty or sixty people. The idol of Lord Jagannath was placed in the middle, richly attired and gorgeously adorned, conveyed from one temple to another. Bernier mentioned that during yatra/march many people were of wild notions as to throw themselves upon the ground in the way of its ponderous wheels which passes over and crushed to atoms the bodies of these extreme devotees. These people did so with the belief that Lord Jagannath would receive them as children and recall them to life in a state of happiness and dignity.

Bernier suspected that the Brahmins promoted those superstitions to which they were indebted for their wealth. They selected a beautiful maiden to become the bride of Jagannath who accompanied the god to the temple with all the pomp and ceremony, where she remained the whole night, having been made to believe that Jagannath would come and lie with her. She was commanded to inquire of the god if the year would be fruitful and what would be the rituals, the festivals, the prayers and the alms which he required in return for his bounty. In the night one of those Brahmins entered the temple through a small back door, enjoyed the unsuspecting damsel, and made her believe whatever may be deemed necessary. The following morning when on her way to another temple, to where she was carried in that Triumphal Chariot, by the side of Jagannath her spouse, she was asked by the Brahmins to state aloud to the people all she had heard from the lustful priest, as every word had proceeded from the mouth of Jagannath.

Funeral Rites

In his book Bernier also reflected on the funeral rights that he attended on the Ganges. According to him, most of the Gentiles burnt their dead; some partially broiled the bodies with stubble, near the side of a river and then precipitate into the water from a high and steep bank. He also observed flights of crows fluttering above the carcass which became as much the prey of those birds as of the fish and the crocodile.

Another way of funeral which he witnessed is that when a person is sick or at the point of death he was carried to the river side, his feet were submerged in the water and was left to get sink gradually to the neck. When it was perceived that his last moments have come, his whole body was immersed into the river. The belief of the ceremony was that the soul should be washed off from all impurities which it might have contracted during its abode in the body.

Fakirs/Saints

Bernier also wrote about Fakirs, Derveshes and holy men or Gentile hypocrites of India who lived in a sort of convent, governed by superiors where vows of chastity, poverty and submission were made. They were seen day and night, seated or lying on ashes entirely naked; frequently under the large trees near talabs (Ponds) or in the galleries round the Devras or idol temples. He mentioned bands of naked Fakirs in the territories of some Rajas. Some had frightful hair either hung loosely or tied or twisted round their heads; some carried a club like Hercules; others had a dry and rough tiger skin throne over their shoulders. They walked through the town shamelessly. Females often brought them alms with much devotion, doubtless believing that they were holy personages. Several of the Fakirs undertook long pilgrimages, not only naked but laden with heavy iron chains others stood upright for seven or eight days, without once sitting or lying down and without any other support that might be afforded by leaning forward against a cord for a few hours in the night. Their legs in the meantime were swollen to the size of their thighs. He also discerned many standing steadily, for long durations upon their hands with the head down & feet in the air. The Fakirs exercised painful austerities in the confident hope that they will be Rajas in their renascent state; or if they did not become Rajas, they should be placed in a condition of life capable of more exquisite enjoyment was experienced by sovereign princess. He also mentioned some of the Fakirs that enjoyed the reputation of being peculiarly enlightened saints, perfect Jauguis and really united with God. They lived a secluded life in a remote garden without ever visiting a town. Frequently they were absorbed in profound meditation.

Bernier gave an account of certain Fakirs totally different from the Saints above mentioned. They almost continually perambulated the country, made light of everything, and believed themselves to be possessed of most important secrets. The people imagined that those favoured beings were well acquainted with the art of making gold, and that they could prepare mercury in so admirable a manner that a grain or two swallowed every morning can restore a diseased body to vigorous health, and thus strengthen the stomach that it might feed with avidity, and digest with ease. This was not all. When two of such good Jauguis met, and could be excited to a spirit of emulation, they made such a display of power of Janguisism, that it might well be doubted if Simon Magus, with all his sorceries, ever performed more surprising feats. They told any person his thoughts, caused the branch of a tree to blossom and to bear fruit within an hour, hatched an egg in their bosom in less than fifteen minutes, producing whatever bird may be demanded, and make it fly about the room, and execute many other prodigies. Bernier wrote that he had never been so fortunate as to witness any such marvellous performances.

Bernier described some more Fakirs of a much more agreeable appearance. They walk the streets barefooted and bareheaded, girt with a scarf which hanged down to the knee, and wearing a white cloth which passed under the right arm and goes over the left shoulder in the form of a mantle, but they were without any under garment. They did not beg from shop to shop like many other fakirs but entered freely into the houses of idolaters, where they met with a hearty welcome and a hospitable reception, their presence being esteemed a blessing to the family.

Sati

Sati was a cruel practice of making a widow burn herself alive on the funeral pyre of her dead husband. Bernier witnessed some incidents of Sati. Sati was widely prevalent among the Hindus. Once when Travelling from Ahmedabad to Agra, through the territories of Rajas, Bernier saw a deep pit filled with wood. A dead man and a woman who was alive were seated upon the same pile of wood. Some Brahmins proceeded to set fire to the pile of wood. The pile on which a great quantity of butter and oil was poured, was soon on fire and enveloped in flames. The widow's garments caught fire too. Bernier was surprised that the victim did not betray the slightest indication of pain.

Another dreadful scene of burning of a widow, he saw during his visit from Surat to Persia. He found several Englishmen, Dutchmen & Monsieur Chardin were present at that place. He described whole process that the lady sat down upon the funeral pyre, placed her deceased husband's head in her lap, took up a mashaal and with her own hands lighted the fire.

Bernier discussed and consulted with many people on the subject of Sati and found that the abominable practice was the effect of early & deeply rooted prejudices. Every girl was taught by her mother that it was virtuous &laudable in a wife to mingle her ashes with those of her husband and that no woman of honor would refuse compliance with the established custom.

But not every woman sacrificed herself willingly. Bernier observed a woman who shrank back a few paces from the pit but was mercilessly thrust forward and forced into the fire. The most poignant incident was the one that he witnessed in Lahore where the victim was barely twelve years old. He described the agony of the girl by indicating that she trembled, wept bitterly but was forced and burnt alive.

> "I found it difficult to repress my feelings and to prevent their bursting forth into clamorous and unavailing rage; but restrained by prudential considerations, I contented myself with silently lamenting the abominable superstition of these people, and applied to it the language of the poet, when speaking of Iphigenia, whom her father Agamemnon had offered in sacrifice to Diana" (314)

This quotation (from Lucretius, De Rerum Natura, Book I.82-6,102) has been thus rendered by H.A.J. Munro: 'Whereas on the contrary, often and often, that very religion has given birth to sinful and unholy deeds. Thus in Aulis the chosen chieftains of the Danai, foremost of men, foully polluted with Iphianassa's blood the altar of the Trivian maid. So great the evils to which religion could prompt!' I have substituted the latest critical version, for the one given by Bernier which he took from a Dutch edition of Lucretius.

Bernier mentioned some of the devoted widows who eluded the vigilance of the murderous priests. He was in company of a fair idolator who contrived to save her life by throwing herself upon the protection of the scavengers who assembled on those occasions in considerable numbers, when they learnt that the intended victim was young and beautiful, that her relations were of little note, and that she was to be accompanied by only a few of her acquaintance. Bernier also added that a woman whose courage failed at the sight of the horrid apparatus of death could not hope to pass her days in happiness or to be treated with respect or affection. No individual of the nation would at any time, or under any circumstances, associate with a creature so degraded, who was accounted utterly infamous, and execrated because of the dishonour which her conduct had brought upon the religion of the country.

Many widows had been rescued by the Portuguese, at sea-ports where these people happened to be in superior strength. Bernier criticized all those cruelties and wished for opportunities to exterminate those cursed Brahmins.

Bernier mentioned some more atrocities towards women. In some parts of India, instead of burning the women who determine not to survive their husbands, the Brahmins buried them alive, by slow degrees, up to the throat and when she had been completely choked, cover over the body with earth thrown upon it and tread upon the head.

Bernier was a keen observer of every event he witnessed. He came from a foreign social and cultural environment. His perception towards all above mentioned social customs and religious practices was very different from an Indian. The strange customs practiced in India evoked in him emotions of awe, and many times of grief and anger.

In his own words, "from that superstitious piety and compassion toward the Sun; from that mad and infernal hardihood of women to burn themselves; from those various and frantic practices of the Fakires; from all that fabulous trash of their Beths; was I not justified in taking as a motto to this letter." (348)

As can be concluded in his own words, Bernier found these practices and beliefs engrossing to an extent that he felt compelled to share his observations with his colleagues and other scholars.

References

1. Chapelain was employed by Colbert in 1662 to guide King Louis XIV in his distribution of pensions.
2. A corruption of Vedas, Divine knowledge
3. The sacred tank at Thaneswar, in the Karnal District, situated on the line of the old Mogul road to Lahore-a very ancient place of Hindoo pilgrimage, was considered the centre of the 'Holy Land' of Kurukshetra. During eclipses of the moon, the waters of all other tanks are believed to visit this tank, so that he who bathes in the assembled water obtains the concentrated merit of all possible ablutions.

CHAPTER 13

Narrating Modernity and Globalisation in Small Indian Towns: A Reading of Pankaj Mishra's Travelogue *Butter Chicken in Ludhiana*

Dr. Kiran Deep

Abstract

The present paper attempts a close reading of Pankaj Mishra's famous travelogue *Butter Chicken in Ludhiana: Travels in Small town India* (1995) for mapping the intellectual crossroads where the dynamics of globalisation have joined the forces of modernisation in inducing social change in India. This travelogue describes the gradual yet profound social and cultural changes taking place in small Indian towns in a new context of globalisation i.e. modernisation and cultural hybridisation.

Keywords: Globalisation, Hybridisation, Modernity, Cultural Hybridity

> "Modernity exists in the form of a desire to wipe out whatever came earlier, in the hope of reaching at least a point that could be called a true present, a point of origin that makes a new departure."
>
> Paul de Man

Underscoring the form and function of modernity as an impulse for change, a driving force opening new avenues for change in society and culture, Paul de Man in his article "Literary History and Literary Modernity" argues that Modernism is neither a movement, nor a specific historical period; rather it is a tendency, a mode of life or a way of thinking marked by a desire to change the existing order. No doubt, this change reflects in every aspect of life in modern globalised society in terms of sociological, technological, and economic advancements. As we move into a global century, we find that several aspects of social and economic life are changing rapidly by virtue of the interconnectedness that brings together the corners of the globe. As the world has contracted, the quality of life has changed regardless of the geographical location.

Being an experiential process, globalisation is different for each person. This process of globalisation as "an intensification of global interconnectedness" suggests "a world full of movement and mixture, contact and linkages, and persistent cultural interaction and exchange" (Inda and Rosaldo, 2). The forces of globalisation have invaded into the intimate spaces occupied by individuals and altered their sensibilities to create new set of values, new norms for society and new definitions for culture and identity. These waves of change have a deep impact on the Indian way of life too. In this changing scenario, the interpretation of local and global has led to the reinterpretation of national and cultural identities. The contemporary travel narratives speak volumes about this change, this shift from local to global. As Indrani M. Desai has observed in her article '*Tandoori Pizza: Fluid Culinary/Cultural Identities in Selected Contemporary Indian Travelogues*', "Contemporary Indian travel landscape is composed of the multitude of voices speaking from the diverse ethno-cultural spheres and from the spaces in-between cultures" (1493). To add further, Dr. Desai remarks that these voices reflect changing attitudes to Indian identities – they speak against homogeneity, uniformity and exclusionary structures. They apprehend the fact that identities are fluid as a consequence of cross-cultural exchanges. The present paper attempts a close reading of Pankaj Mishra's famous travelogue *Butter Chicken in Ludhiana: Travels in Small town India* (1995) for mapping the intellectual crossroads where the dynamics of globalisation have joined the forces of modernisation in inducing social change in India. Through this travelogue, Mishra attempts a sharp insight into the minds of the people all around India. With the aim of depicting India in transition, Mishra describes the lives of various everyday people all through a huge undercurrent of economic and social change which in turn is changing the quality of people's values, customs, hopes and dreams. This travelogue describes the gradual yet profound social and cultural changes taking place in small Indian towns in the new context of globalisation. It brings vividly to life nineteen small towns of India, describing them not in exotic or quaint terms, but rather in the frightening new context of modernisation and globalisation. More interestingly even if he visits a famous tourist destination, he awaits a different situation as he talks about his trip to Simla: – "Towards the end of October, I went to Simla and found it cleansed of tourists, and restored to its permanent residents."(1)

Being an insider with an Indian perspective Mishra sets up his route through small towns. However, compared with some other travelogues ever written about India it is this choice which makes the key difference. Mishra sets up his itinerary on small towns which seems an unusual decision when one thinks about the large Indian subcontinent with all its attractions to exert a pull on a traveler's desire. His observations are concentrated on the people in small Indian towns and he highlights the transformations which they have undergone due to the influence of Western cultures. To quote Somdatta Mandala:

> "Travel writing is also the art of discovering the magic of ordinary people, places and things. You can discover magic only if you can look beyond reality to the reality behind everything……the urge to travel was built in our genes, driven by the magic of curiosity." (1)

Mishra has tried to show the effects of economic liberalisation and cultural social modernisation at a newer scale: small towns as the smaller cells of a grand community like India. The focus is on small towns and no distinct places are taken into consideration in these towns unless they relate to the main objective of the narrative i.e. depicting social, cultural, and economic transformations of a nation as part of modernity and globalisation. In order to map out the travelogue, we find out that writer's journey starts from Simla at North, goes on to Jaipur at East, continues to Kanyakumari at far South and ends in Jehanabad at West. There are also some other towns in between. We can formulate the outcomes of these trips when each small picture is put beside one another; the way a jigsaw puzzle is done. Then it is only with the big picture in view that one can accomplish a better understanding of the themes and motifs of the book. Mishra himself declares in the Prologue, "…small, scattered details were meaningless in themselves. It was only when they were seen together that a coherent picture emerged"(xii)

Mishra presents various characters who try to mimic the Western culture to become modern. He highlights how the mindset of the people even in the small towns of India is deeply affected by the Western intrusion. The characters in *Butter Chicken in Ludhiana* often move back and forth between the West and the East in their dreams or in their real life as they wish for fulfillment in both cultures. The cultural clashes, quest for identity and longing for a better life-style in the swiftly changing world form the main content in this travel narrative.

This travel narrative opens with a description of Simla. Mishra observed that people visited Simla initially to enjoy the natural beauty of the place but the situation had changed with time. When he was in Simla, he had noticed that people would come and watch the beautiful sunset in silence and quickly after that they would rush to break the oppressive silence by indulging their tastes in the modern set up. People's interests had changed. They now wanted to enjoy the busy urban life in the malls and video game parlours. To quote Mishra,

> "The tourists would stand and stare perplexedly for a few seconds, and then they would be in a hurry to leave, to flee the oppressive silence and solitude, and go back to Simla wherein beckoned the Mall's colourful bustle, the Beautiful People from Chandigarh – the petulant Punjabi beauties and their strapping young squires – the video-game parlours, the hotels with their naughty cable offerings of new Hindi movies, and the shops blaring out the hits of the summer." (1)

Mishra talks about a Mr. Bannerji whom he met during a bus journey when he was at Simla. Mr. Bannerjiis presented as a modern man who had overcome his patriarchal attitude. He mimicked the Western mannerisms but sometimes he failed to do so. While talking to Pankaj Mishra he tried to present himself as a sophisticated and modern individual. He conversed with Pankaj Mishra about politics in Jawaharlal Nehru University and was very curious that Pankaj Mishra was a student of Jawaharlal Nehru University. In the meantime, he struggled to maintain his posture. "Luckily, after some time Mr. Banerji found his posture too painful to maintain. He turned his back, and, finally, fell silent" (13). He got really irritated by the obscene music which was being played in the bus and shouted for the music to be stopped. When the younger people, some honeymooners in the bus began to rebel for the song to be kept on played, Mr. Banerji became quiet.

This incompatibility between two generations is highlighted through the example of Mr. Sharma's family whom Pankaj Mishra met at Ambala. There would be many people like Mr. Sharma belonging to the older generation who cannot simply change according to the changing times. Mishra also portrays Mrs. Sharma and their daughters Kavita and Neha. Even though Mr. Sharma seemed to be old fashioned, his daughters were modern in all sense. For example, during the1980s Camay soap was not very common in India and it was imported and highly priced. When Dharma Kumar used Mr. Sharma's daughter, Neha's soap, she shouts angrily: "Who has been using my Camay Soap?!! Does anyone in this house care that I buy it from my pocket money?!! Does anyone care?!" (47-48). Mr. Sharma's daughters were trying to convince others that they were not like their father, but they were entirely modern and their way of talking and behaviour supported their attitude. This family is a typical example of a middle-class Indian family influenced by the West, trying to mimic the West. In the postcolonial period, people thought that their pride and glory were heightened when behaved like the Western people.

Mishra's visit to Jaipur also reveals for him "symbols of India's shabby modernity" (54). The Jaipur that Mishra had visited when he was young was an elegant place at that time. He opines that Jaipur was "the most well-planned of all old cities in India" (53). But on a later visit he found that it had changed beyond recognition. He felt that modernity had lowered the standard of living there. Through the description of Jaipur, a clear picture of modernisation and its resultant corruption is presented. Mishra tries to reclaim the glory of past by exploring what has been lost.

Being an insider, Pankaj Mishra's travel memoirs often compare the past glory and the modern hybrid culture of Indian towns. He had already travelled to most of these places when he was young and therefore, he writes about the change which he saw in those places. He opines that the past glory and beauty of most of the places in India is lost when the people are craving for modernity. Pushkar, in Rajasthan, is cited as a place which has lost its serene and sacred atmosphere after Westernisation. Pushkar was like "a mini Haridwar, with shops selling flowers, coconuts, conch -shells, framed calendar-art pictures of divinities and barfis for prasad." (58). But now, Mishra sadly narrates "the town itself entirely belied my expectations." (58). In the present Pushkar, "The narrow alleys were still there, but they resembled not those of Hardwar or Benares, but of Thamel, Kathmandu. There were multi-cuisine restaurants with menus displayed on small boards outside in German, Italian, French, not English." (58) And so, this travelogue talks about the waves of liberalisation and socio-cultural modernisation which have changed the life in small towns of India after the colonial period.

During his travels, Mishra observed that English language is one of the major influences on the people of India, even in the small villages or towns. The people, whom Mishra conversed with, were trying to talk both in English and in their native language. Most of the dialogues between Mishra and the natives were in English and its translation in the native language can also be found. Along with fascination for English language, fashion from the movies and fashion shows on the TV had great influence on the people of India. By organising fashion shows with an interest in modelling, they try to imitate or mimic the Western cultures. There is a mixture of both cultures located in Bhabha's 'Third Space' where different cultures meet. Mishra writes about Mrs. Shukla and her daughter Rita whom he had met on the train at Jhansi. Mrs. Shukla was escorting her daughter to Mumbai where they believe a fashion career awaited her and she would become a model. Mrs. Shukla was very excited to share with her fellow passengers the future that awaited her daughter. She feels it is time, "now for Indian women to throw off their chains. You look at these fashion programmes on STAR PLUS-how confident and bold those models are. Even though, they are not beautiful. Why can't we become like that? After all, Indian women are the most beautiful in the world. Why don't we show our beauty on the world stage?' (132)

Like Mrs. Sharma's daughter Neha at Ambala or Mrs. Shukla's daughter Rita at Jahnsi, Mishra has many more young people in his memories whom he met during his travels, who try to mimic the Western ways to prove themselves modern. This approach towards life brings in the question of identity crisis which many people seem to be experiencing at the moment. Rapid social changes are the cause of disintegration of most of the homogenous and stable identity designs, and the result is the emergence of the concept of multiple identities created across cultural, ethnic and other borders. New identity and ethnicity formations have become an invariable part of lives in multicultural societies. Since multiculturalism as a policy appears to limit identities and expressions of ethnicity, trans-culturalism can become a suitable approach because it has a capacity to promote reformulation of cultural identities which suit the rapidly changing contexts. The main factor leading to the identity crisis include the breaking up of most of the all-encompassing identity schemes such as family or nation, great demographic shifts, or forces of globalisation in tension with local pressures. New identities stemming from this situation are hybrid and fluid. Identity has become decentered, ambivalent and contextual. Mishra makes an association between economic globalisation and ethical, social and cultural problems experienced by the people. This happens when he comes to know that some hotels at Kovalam Beach do not admit Indians. As Mishra remarks:

> But India wasn't a tourist economy – at least, not yet. All the more disturbing, then, it was to know about places where the shoddy practice of poor parasitic nations had crept in. In India, they were an unpleasant reminder of old colonial hierarchies: whites at the top, Indians somewhere at the bottom, finding their own different levels of degradation. They spoke, at least in certain quarters, of the growing damage, after just forty-seven years of independence, to national self-esteem; and they were the unexplored darker side of globalisation. (167).

The age of transnational and post-national identity seems to have set in and every national identity seems to be in a process of assimilation and transformation. The comforting images of nation, national language, and coherent communities are no longer sufficient. The English movies were a great influence on the younger generation. Mishra talks about a ten-year-old boy whom he met at a marriage ceremony at Hapur. At the first glance, his use of English and the Malcolm X cap presented his inclination towards the West. He experienced the same at Bangalore which is known for its cultural pluralism. He writes, "The appurtenances of modernity were conspicuous: the kids in Reeboks and Nikes, chewing Wrigley's chewing gum, clamouring to be taken to Spencer's open-air café. Yuppies, in loosened ties, sipping lager beer, talking stock-market jargon at Rice Bowl…." (141)

Kottayam in Kerala is also presented as a small place which was ahead of the expectation of Mishra. In Kottayam, he could find many 'boutiques' with an international look. The readymade clothes shop called themselves as 'boutique'. Mishra spots the alien setting of these shops, "these shops with their clean-cut lines, their dust-free interiors, their glass fronts, their air-conditioning, created an oppressively unfamiliar world for their inhabitants in a small place like Kottayam (157). When Mishra saw these shops, and he was reminded of the first 'fast-food' restaurant that had opened in Allahabad in 1987. The owner of the restaurant was inspired by a shop in Delhi named "Nirula", which was in turn inspired by

'McDonald's'. The owner of the shop recreated 'Nirula' in Allahabad. But both the shops in Allahabad and Delhi looked very strange and unfamiliar that a few customers did not even step inside because of the fear of being embarrassed. Mishra also describes the staff in these shops who were mostly the local people as being very uncomfortable in "their alien Americanised surroundings, always looking, in their jaunty peaked caps and monogrammed uniforms, like people trapped in an overly elaborate and pointless masquerade" (158).

Not only the common people, but also personalities like Mrs. Mary Roy, a famous litigant and the Principal of Corpus Christi School in Kottayam are presented as persons who want to have a modern identity. In Kottayam, she had a stable existence but the deadening impact of her surroundings made her re-think her existence. She wondered at Pankaj Mishra's interest in Kottayam, "It is such a backward small town. Nothing happens here." (160) This was the reason why she sent her daughter out of Kottayam. She did not want her daughter to grow up in a backward place like Kottayam. When Mishra mentions his visit to the readymade shops he visited, her thoughts, her love for being modern suddenly take a turn and she says, "Oh! Kottayam is a very modern place. You'd be surprised. All these people are incredibly rich." (160)

And so, Pankaj Mishra's reflections on the way middle-class people in small -towns of India live with their aspirations to be modernised and struggle hard to be in tune with western way of life leaves an answered question – 'Is this Homi K. Bhabha's "Third Space of Enunciation" (156)or a dark zone of imitation and pretension?' Indeed, this fluidity and hybridity of global communities demand new definitions, new vocabulary as it is projected through the life at small towns of India in Mishra's engaging travel narrative, *Butter Chicken in Ludhiana: Travels in Small Town India.*

References

Bhabha, Homi K. "Cultural Diversity and Cultural Differences," *The Post-Colonial Studies Reader*, ed. B. Ashcroft, G. Griffiths, H. Tiffin, Routledge, New York 2006.

Desai, Indrani M. "Tandoori Pizza: Fluid Culinary/Cultural Identities in Selected Contemporary Indian Travelogues". *European Academic Research.* Vol.III, Issue2/ May 2005.

https://www.euacademic.org/UploadArticle/1624.pdf

Inda, Jonathan X. and Renato Rosaldo. "Introduction." *The Anthropology of Globalization: A Reader.* Malden, MA: Blackwell Publishers Inc., 2002.

Man Paul De. "Literary History and Literary Modernity". *Blindness and Insight: Essays in the Rhetoric of Contemporary Criticism.* London: Routledge, 1983.

Mandal, Somdatta.Editorial Introduction: *India and Travel Narratives.* Rupkatha *Journal on Interdisciplinary Studies in Humanities.* Vol. 12, No. 3, 2020

https://dx.doi.org/10.21659/rupkatha.v12n3.00

Mishra, Pankaj. *Butter Chicken in Ludhiana: Travels in Small Town India.* Gurugram: Penguin Random House India, 2006.

CHAPTER 14

Pilgrimage as a Medium of Portrayal of Society: An Analysis of Chauser's *The Prologue to the Canterbury Tales*

Guman Singh Gehlot

Abstract

Journey, in any form, whether it is a pilgrimage or travel to a place has been a kind of passion or venture to seek or to learn about new places and people. The sojourner not only learns about the newer things he comes to, he explores his inner world as well. Journey becomes a medium to recognise the truths of life. In this manner, at metaphorical level we say that life is a journey. Chaucer, in his "The Prologue to the Canterbury Tales" has employed the idea of pilgrimage to portray the character of contemporary society. He brings together people from different walks of life ranging from the sacred to the secular, and the profane. The characters are timeless and temporal. Chaucer, with the help of irony and juxtaposition suggests the hollowness and hypocrisy of contemporary times which can be identified in modern society too.

Keywords: Journey, spiritual terms, Human Comedy, Pilgrimage, Criticism of life, Sacred, Secular, Profane.

The journey to the shrine of St. Thomas A. Beckett is, to a metaphorical level, is a journey to the inner recesses of contemporary times. In spiritual terms it symbolises the stumbling life long journey of imperfect people towards death, sinning and failing but also praying and journeying in faith. That all the portraits in The Prologue to the Canterbury Tales are portraits of pilgrims needs no defense. Most of the religious festivities all over the world begin around the months of March or April – a fact which Sir J. G. Frazer would readily testify and Chaucer begins the Prologue with

> "Whan that Aprille with his shouressote
> The droghte of Marche hath perched to the rote"

The Prologue begins with an idea of procreation in terms of seasons – the female March and the male -April, and the marriage of water and earth. The Prologue treats pilgrimage first as an event in the calender of nature and proceeds to suggest the renewal of human mobility, energy and wayfaring. The spectroscope narrows down from a vision of the strange and faraway to a specific pilgrimage, and finally to the shrine at Canterbury. The Canterbury pilgrimage is a manifestation, therefore, of the tide of life whose ebb and flow responds to the pilgrimage which is also some sort of an annual ritual.

> This world nis but a thurghfareful of wo,
> And we ben pilgrims, passinge to and fro.
>
> (Knight's Tale)

The use of a pilgrimage as the framing device enabled Chaucer to bring together people from different walks of life: Knight, Prioress, Monk, Pardoner, Wife of Bath, Miller, Merchent, Frankling, Clerk of Oxford, Man of Law, Reeve and a host of other characters. A way of life, and a civilisation different in many respects from our own – though our own has evolved from it – goes to the composing of that Chaucerian depth. The human comedy of the Canterbury Tales moves within an apprehension of an all – inclusive divine harmony. There is no mitigation of the evil in the Canterbury pilgrims nor in the characters of their tales; indeed, have the rogues and scoundrels been remarked to predominate in the Canterbury Tales.

The portraits offer us a range of motivation – from the sacred to the secular, and the profane. The unity of Canterbury Tales lies in that all the pilgrims are granted a sacred motive, the journey to the Canterbury Shrine. But the range of motivations within the overall motivation varies. The motivation of Knight, the parson, the wife of Bath, represents one side; the motivation of Summoner and the Pardoner represents the other side. The Wife of Bath's tale is secular and profane than sacred though still a part of the pilgrimage. The prayer for purification of motive is valid for all pilgrims, however, has the restlessness and the self-imposed compulsions of a mystic in his or her search for Truth or God. The gathering is social, the motivation general. All move in a procession because the pilgrimage is there; we are not told what had happened or how pilgrims behaved when they reached the shrine, or which of them encountered reality. We are simply given a description of the journey and the journey –

men and women. There is nothing specifically religious about the motley crowd.

The knight, the Squire and their attendant Yeoman evidently form a group, a distinct element in this community. The rather faded, crusading Knight is felt as already passing into the past, to be remembered for an inner beauty of life beneath his battered exterior expressed in the tenderly nostalgic line.

He was a verrayparfitgentil Knight

An inner beauty of life is felt as shared by several among the least externally distinct figures in the procession, the Knight, the Poor Parson and his brother the Plowman –

Livinge in pees and parfitcharitee.

It cannot be accidental that the Knight has this quality in common with the plowman; they are blood-brothers in Christ.

The immediate contrast to the ageing Knight is his son, the young squire, the eternal young bachelor (Sir Mirthe and Youthe), an extravagant spring – like figure – the new generation – but truly accomplished and courtly.

Embrouded was he, as it were a mede
Al ful of fresh he floures, whyte and rede.

The external fadedness of the Knight is emphasised by this sharp contrast with the gay extravagance of the young squire and with the specter Robin – Hood like apparition of the Yeoman who is, underneath simply a solid English countryman.

But Chaucer's most serious 'criticism of life' in the Prologue is implied in his presentation of the ecclesiastics. The art is in seeing exactly what each is in relation to what each ought to be; an art of exact contemplation but not in a void. The art is as much in what is left unsaid as in what is said, with simple juxtaposition of statements. It is in the presentation of the Prioress that the most delicately poised irony is apprehensible.

That of hirsmyling was ful simple and coy;
Hirgrettesteooth was but by seynt Loy;
And she was cleped madam Eglentyne.
Fulwel she song the service divine;
Entuned in hir nose fulsemely.

Her 'smylingful simple and coy' already suggests a young girl in the presence of young men rather than a prioress. The name Eglentyne, a wild rose, is also a little unexpected as a name for a prioress. Her table manners not only show that she has been genteelly brought up, their dainty ritual and nicety overelaborated, in one dedicated after all to the rigour of the monastic life. Her anxiety to 'ben holdendigne of reverence' by affectation of courtly manners rather than by holiness of life confirms the underlying note of worldly vanity.

The irony implied in the presentation of the Monk depends on a less ambiguous contrast between his grosser worldliness and his monastic profession. This hunting Monk is one of those lords of creation who ride across all the rules; his bridle's profane sound rivals the chapel bell.

Chaucer, no doubt delightedly appreciates the Monk as a fine specimen, a rich *ensample*, but that he does not approve of him the irony most clearly indicates.

> Gerhoundes he hadde, as swifte as fowel in fight.
> Of priking and of hunting for the hare
> Was all his lust, for no cost wolde he spare.

Unlike the Prioresse's *Amor Vincit Omnia*, the signification of the love – knot at the end of the gold pin which fastens the Monk's hood under his chin is not in doubt. The distinct visualisation shows us well cared for, over – indulged, pampered body.

> His need was balled, that shoon as any glas.
> And eek his face, as he had been anoint.

'As he had been anoint' contains within itself a contrast between the holy oil and his greasy fatness; 'in good point', as might be said as of a horse or dog, implies his animality. The irony is concentrated in the final ambiguity –

> Now certainly he was a fair prelat which confirms the irony right at the beginning
> A Manly man, to been an abbot able.
> In what sense is he 'a fair prelat'?
> Now certainly he was fair prelat; He was not pale as a for – pynedgoost.
> A Fat swan loved he best of any roost.

This Lover of good feeding and good hunting is 'fair' in the worldly, the corporal, not spiritual sense.

The Friar, again seen simply as what and for what he is makes a broader implied contrast with what he ought to be. The traditional themes of covetousness and abuse of confession, the more outrageous in one vowed to celibacy, form the basic moral pattern of the 'character'. His human relationships are determined not by his religious obligations, which would direct him to 'lazars' and 'beggesteres', but, like those of Fals – semblant, by his gluttony.

He knew the taverneswel in every town,
And everichhostiler and tappestere
Better than a lazar or a beggestere;

His predatory covetousness exploits the charity of those who are themselves in direct need of charity.

For there he was not lyk a cloisterer,
With a thredbar cope, as is a pourescoler,
But he was lyk a maister or a pope.

Then there are characters engaged in diverse secular occupations, mostly of the new 'middle class' which was emerging in the towns of Chaucer's England. They give an impression of a rich diversity of human folk. The Seven Deadly Sins continue to nourish the roots of the subtle individual characterisation; thus Gluttony underlies the Frankeleyn, Avarice the Doctor of Phisyk. There is a grave discrepancy between the appearance the Merchant keeps up and what lies behind the appearance.

Therwiste no wight that he was in dette.
The Man of Lawe, too, keeps up an elaborate pretence. No – Wher so bisy a man as he thernas,
And yet he semed bister than he was.

He is busy about many vain things; like the Marchant, he seems wiser than he is.

He seemed swich, his wordesweren so wyse.

His accumulated legal learning has only a cash value for him. In short, the Merchant and the Man of Lawe are both worldly men in contrast to the Clerk of Oxenford, the unworldly scholar of all time.

The Frankeleyn is one of the most vivid of the secular figures.
Whyt was his berd, as is the dayesye.
Of his complexioun he was sangwyn.

Ruddiness of colour is, of course, a secondary implication of 'sangwyncomplexioun'; yet it seems likely that the visual impression – ruddy 'complexion' in the modern sense – is an immediately relevant one here in contrast to the white beard.

The most vivid of all the secular figures is the Wife of Bath. The critical irony accompanying her presentation depends again on the contrast, in relation to her, between formal religious observance and profane impulse.

In at the parisshewyf ne was ther noon.
That to th' offringbiforehirsholde goon;
And if therdide, cesteyn, so wrooth was she,
That she was out of allecharitee.

'Charitee' is the key word of the irony here, as 'conscience' is at one point the presentation of the Prioresse. Her uncharitablenes in church, proceeds from Pride which at this point, in her own unique way, she typifies. She must go before, in that respect have the 'maïstrye'; and it is especially on Sunday of all days that her vanity flares out, is flaunted in flamboyant costume.

Hircoverchiefsfulfyne were of ground;
I dorsteswere the weyedenten pound
That on a Sonday were upon hir heed.
Hir hosen weren of fyn scarlet reed,
Fulstreite y - teyd, and shoes fulmoiste and newe.

The Wife is a new social type, an exuberant ensample of the newly opulent, ostentations cloth – making bourgeoisie – though her costume is amusingly not quite the height of fashion. In spite of her loud dress and manner, she is realised as a humanly attractive as well as a dazzling figure, a gay, talkative, formidable, dominating person.

Bold was her face, and fair, and reed of hewe.
She was a worthy woman all hirlyve,
Housbondes at chirche – dove she haddefyve,
Withouten other companye in youthe.

Parallel with her many amorous adventures are her many far pilgrimages; she is restless, adventurous, curious.

She coude much of wandring by the weye.

The Summoner and the Pardoner who conclude the Tales are distortions in relation to the profession they are supposed to uphold.

The former is lecherous, the latter is an eunuch. Their song, which ought to relate to the song divine, is an exercise in dramatic irony.

Chaucer has succeeded in letting an ideal emerge from most of his portraits in spite of the drawbacks they have. The ideal may still be imbued with irony but that does not distort its being an ideal. For example, as we have seen the Friar and the Pardoner are condemned for corruption but there is always an image of the worthy Friar and a Pardoner who was a noble ecclesiastic in the light of which chaucer is evaluating his portraits.

The pilgrims share destructive and restorative aspects of love; barring few, the pilgrims are worldly; the purpose of Chaucer being to mock the idea of the journey and the journeymen. None of the characters is made to sing or talk of the stories relating to Christ. Most of the characters are finely dressed, care more for their physical lineaments than for the sermon. Christ asked to give up earthly possessions, while the pilgrims (characters) take delight in them, Chaucer has made the idea of pilgrimage a means to interpret his comic vision through the galaxy of character – portraits. The background design, nevertheless, remains that of a pilgrimage. The Summoner and the Pardoner do suggest acts of summoning and pardoning; the feelings of expatiation which such acts suggest round out a Christian poem. The satire and irony, latent almost throughout in Canterbury Tales, are given saving graces by the very idea of pilgrimage, which, though, satirised, is still a pilgrimage through which God receives his devotees and grants them grace.

References

1. Cawley, A.C. *Geoffrey Chaucer: Canterbury Tales,* London: David Campbell Publishers Ltd., 1992.
2. Chaucer, Geoffrey. *The Riverside Chaucer.* London: Oxford University Press, 2008.
3. Chauces, Geoffrey, *The Canterbury Tales,* trans. N. Coghill. New York: Penguin Classics, 1977. Print.
4. Brewer, D. S. *Chaucer's Mind and Art*, Edinburg, 1969.
5. Coulton, G. G. *Chaucer & his England*, London, Methuen,1963.
6. Speirs, John, *Chaucer the Maker*, Faber & Faber Ltd., London, 1982.
7. Sullivan, Sheila, *Critics on Chaucer*, George Allen and Unwin Ltd., London, 1970.
8. Trevelyan, G. M. *English Social History*, Orient Longman Ltd., Green & Co., New York, 1994.

CHAPTER 15

Marlowe as the Narrator in the *Heart of Darkness*: As Agent of Civilisation and Against Primitivism

Dr. Ranjit Kaur

Abstract

Heart of Darkness is about moral and political issues, and in order to convey them, it is clear that a new method must be found. The issues must be put, and they are put by Marlow, the narrator of the story. *Heart of Darkness* begins with the first narrator introducing to the four persons on board the Nellie, a cruising yawl: the Director, the Lawyer, the Accountant, and Marlow. They are waiting for the turn of the tide on the River Thames. Marlow's function is to comment. He is, of course, a sub-division of Conrad's personality, objectified for the added sociability of enabling the author to converse with himself. He shares Conrad's fundamental outlook and a complete whole as a character not a puppet. The story of *Heart of Darkness*, according to Guerard, is primarily about Marlow, though it calls into question the extent to which Marlow's night journey is congruent with Conrad's own journey to the Congo and its significance for him. The so-called "unspeakable" terms with which Marlow conveys his experience in the African jungle, may be specific terms in Marlow's meditation; this forms a part of Marlow's character. This article attempts to discuss the aspect of Marlow's whimsical indirection, fragmentation, hesitancy, and the like, tend to increase as he proceeds up the river. The article tries to find out Why Have a Narrator at All? And focuses on how Marlow assumes a middle-of-the-road position on everything and seeks to mediate between the extremes; in this, he embodies the British spirit of compromise. In this novella, he mediates between the illusioned, sentimental innocence and the complex Satanism of Kurtz himself, between the light of civilisation and the darkness of primitivism, between colonialising Europe and exploited Africa.

Keywords: Journey, Narrator, Unspeakable, Civilisation, Primitivism

Why Have a Narrator at All?

The first question to ask is why have a narrator at all? Henry James has some interesting points to make about this question. In his prefaces, he discusses how a writer can extract maximum significance from his material, he often stresses the necessity of choosing a particular kind of spectator. He stresses the need for "a reflecting and colouring medium." His point is that it is better to refract the unusual through the normal, to make the alien and remote pass through the near and recognisable, to bring the extraordinary event to us via an ordinary sensibility – because this way you ensure a maximum of mental and emotional involvement. If we were simply told the facts of Kurtz's life, we might feel sorry for him, but as we watched him, haunted, bemused, and alone, we should never feel ourselves involved in his predicament. We should remain disengaged and feel ourselves to be a little superior. But to remain outside the circle of Marlow's auditors is impossible. He professes a range of values that are too central, civilized, and humane to permit any disaffiliation on our part. His doubts and questions, his speculations and assertions, his tolerance, his memory, and his understanding of human behavior – all these things identify us with the story. We are with Marlow, committed to the quality of his mind. And because Marlow feels curiously involved with Kurtz, the whole problem of Kurtz's conduct gradually puzzles, implicates, and challenges us. We watch Kurtz through his eyes, not for vicarious thrills and adventures, but for the generally relevant psychological truths to be revealed.

To get at the full significance of Kurtz, Conrad moves warily and musingly around his accumulated material, listening to many voices, soliciting different opinions, and comparing many peripheral experiences. And to achieve these effects Conrad had to abandon his omniscient viewpoint of things and exploit the strategy of the involved narrator. The story of *Heart of Darkness* is about moral and political issues, and in order to convey them, it is clear that a new method must be found. The issues must be put, and they are put by Marlow, the narrator of the story.

ow's Functions as a Narrator

Heart of Darkness begins with the first narrator introducing to the four persons on board the Nellie, a cruising yawl: the Director, the Lawyer, the Accountant, and Marlow. They are waiting for the turn of the tide on the River Thames. Marlowe is presented as sitting cross-legged like the meditating Buddha; which indicates that he is highly imaginative and unworldly. He looks inward rather than outward. After introducing Marlow and the other three persons on board the Nellie, the first narrator disappears from the scene, and in his place, Marlow takes charge of the narration.

Marlow's function is to comment. He is, of course, a sub-division of Conrad's personality, objectified for the added sociability of enabling the author to converse with himself. He shares Conrad's fundamental outlook and a complete whole as a character not a puppet. A comment is necessary since Conrad could not draw a character from the inside; he could not dramatize another man's mind. "He could not invent. He could not see things which were not, or never had been, before his eyes. His whole magnificent perceptiveness depended absolutely on the senses." Given the smallest core of facts, he could penetrate, illuminate, and fix its significance.

In all the novels in which he appears, Marlow is a detective of the human soul; in *Heart of Darkness*, he follows clues toward solving the mystery of Kurtz. Both in *Heart of Darkness* and *Lord Jim*, Marlow suffers a mental crisis, in one through his encounter with Kurtz, in the other through catching sight of Jim. Kurtzs' soul is not the essence of the plot. Kurtz is not interesting so much in himself as in what made him. Marlow is forever fusing about reality and unreality, but it is his own rather than his listeners' faculties that he, mistrusts. We are cautioned at the start that Marlow will see the meaning of the episode "only as a glow brings out a haze." And still this Marlow identifies himself with his English listeners to the point of assuming that they will see in the story neither less nor more than he sees himself. His listeners accept this in silence.

The story of *Heart of Darkness*, according to Guerard, is primarily about Marlow, though it calls into question the extent to which Marlow's night journey is congruent with Conrad's own journey to the Congo and its significance for him. Although Conrad seems to disappear into Marlow, he remains detached. The best clues he gives to this separateness are in the incremental repetitions of which Marlow is not fully cognizant, and the self-contradictions into which Marlow stumbles again and again without noticing.

In all the stories in which he appears, Marlow must be taken as a choral character in the fullest sense-for all practical purposes the voice of Conrad himself. Marlow's meditative history-not the train of physical events reflected in that history-must be taken as the reader's primary object of interest. He is a seaman in a world where shipboard society is a symbol of all human life: his motives are never commercial or merely prudential, but rather spiritual; he combines a learned vocabulary with the skepticism and irony of hard experience; he has voyaged alone to dark places and returned to tell the tale, and he provides the reader a moral framework for his tale.

An important feature of both *Youth* and *Heart of Darkness*, for example, is the exact composition of Marlow's audience, and their reaction to his tale. In both cases, the audience represents a spectrum of social types and values; implicit in their appreciation of Marlow is an admission that his point of view somehow transcends their own partial ones. To brighten this spotlighting of Marlow and divert attention from the personalities of his auditors to their functions as representatives of a moral spectrum, Conrad refrains from giving them names "the man of finance, the man of accounts, the man of law" have the further status of having been seamen, so that their grudging nods of agreement with Marlow are even more significant; and their final acknowledgment of the meaning of his tale, as in the famous last sentence of *Heart of Darkness*, acts as a powerful persuasion on the reader.

Marlow assumes a middle-of-the-road position on everything and seeks to mediate between the extremes; in this, he embodies the British spirit of compromise. In this novella, he mediates between the illusioned, sentimental innocence and the complex Satanism of Kurtz himself, between the light of civilisation and the darkness of primitivism, between colonialising Europe and exploited Africa. He is, throughout, the supreme compromiser, the moderator of the show who yet does not renounce his own views; his role as a technician is constantly reinforced and humanised by his private apparatus of moral opinion and amateur philosophising. More than anything else, Marlow is the conscience of the community, with whom all its members are involved as communicants. He is a Don Quixote who has lived long enough to change, an Idealist turned empiricist, a romanticist turned ironist.

Marlow: The Moral Participant

Marlow, the narrator, is the moral participant in this novella. The moral darkness of Africa, we learn later, is not the simple darkness of native "ignorance", but of Whiteman who have blinded themselves and corrupted the natives by their claim to be light-bearers. Compared with the English conquests, Marlow claims, the Roman conquests of England were "just robbery with violence aggravated murder on a grand scale, and men going at it blind as is very proper for those who tackle a darkness." But Conrad's heart through Marlow's mouth offers an unambiguous apology for British imperialism. He will himself finally say that he had to lay the ghost of Kurtz's "gifts" with a lie, but it is left to the reader to perceive that Marlow must kill off a part of his own self-knowledge with lies in order to save the "beautiful world" of British civilisation along with the beautiful world of Kurtz's Intended. As the novella progresses, Marlow and Kurtz become involved in a close personal relationship. Marlow ceases to be an observer and becomes a participant in Kurtz's fate.

Marlow's Personality: An Unworldly and Meditative Figure

In *Heart of Darkness*, Marlow is first seen sitting "cross-legged right aft, leaning against the mizzenmast. He had sunken cheeks, a yellow complexion, a straight back, an ascetic aspect, and, with his arms dropped, the palms of hands outwards, resembled an idol;" at the end, he is found once again "in the pose of a meditating Buddha." Some attempt has been made to read Marlow's experience in light of these Oriental suggestions; however, valid this reading, Marlow is at least depicted as an outwardly and meditative figure in the highest sense. His posture contrasts sharply with that of the Director, standing in a nautical pose looking seaward; or the Lawyer, lying comfortably cushioned on deck; or the Accountant, toying with the mathematical bones from his domino box. Marlow's gaze is inward. His abstraction from the physical world is complete. His first speech – "And this also has been one of the dark places of the earth" – emerges suddenly, as if conjoined with some silent meditation. The Oriental overtones give us the impression that Marlow has a kind of wisdom more ancient than the Renaissance wisdom implicit in the first narrator's rhapsody on the Thames. Again, these Oriental overtones set him apart from his thoroughly English audience.

He is the bachelor, the wanderer, the uninvited guest, and the seaman superior to his class, and the teller-of-tales, whose sensibility and purity of judgment intrigue and exasperate his auditors. "The meaning of Marlow's stories, says the frame narrator of *Heart of*

Darkness is like 'one of these misty halos that sometimes are made visible by the spectral illumination of the moonshine" a piece of ironic diffidence on Conrad's part which suggests that the 'adjectival vagueness' of parts of *Heart of Darkness* is intentional, and places those readers who object to that "vagueness" in the same *class* with Marlow's auditors: more accustomed to tales which have a direct simplicity, the whole meaning of which lies within the shell of a cracked nut.'

The so-called "unspeakable" terms with which Marlow conveys his experience in the African jungle, may be specific terms in Marlow's meditation; this forms a part of Marlow's character. Marlow's whimsical indirection, fragmentation, hesitancy, and the like, tend to increase as he proceeds up the river.

Marlow: The Agent of Civilisation against Primitivism

Like Kurtz, Marlow is also the agent of civilisation against primitivism. Civilised men have to plunge into contact with the primitive-their own primitive selves as well as primitive societies-before they can get to the bottom of their own natures, but they must not linger there too long. If they do, they may become prey to satanic temptations like Kurtz in the heart of his African darkness. Marlow follows Kurtz to his final station, hears his last words, and serves as his spiritual executor by bringing back his body and delivering the last message to his grieving sweetheart, but returns to Europe before he himself sinks irretrievably into the Kurtzian quagmire. He undertakes a long journey to the Inner Station in the African jungle to meet and talk to Kurtz, but the static, airless, primitive atmosphere of the Inner Station begins to suffocate him, and he can hardly wait to get back to the civilised world "where events move, men change, light flickers, life flows in a clear stream, no matter whether over mud or over stones."

Marlow's Humanity

Marlow embraces the inescapable darkness of life, but it is a mark of his humanity that he maintains his powers of discrimination within it. He discovers that it is possible to function in darkness without falling satanically into its bottomless pit like Kurtz, or existing like the manager, without the slightest awareness of light. He maintains himself by continually making moral judgments about the experience before him. He recognises the young Russian as admirable incarnation of youthful adventurousness, just as the manager's assistant, with his nose for influential connections back home, is a "papier-mâché Mephistopheles." He admires the company's chief accountant who, in the grueling heat of Africa, appears in starched collar, white cuffs, and snowy trousers: "in the great demoralisation of the land, he kept up his appearance."

Along the coast Marlow observes a boat being paddled by blacks, He admires their wild vitality, their intense energy of movement. That Marlow is a human being becomes candidly clear from his reaction at the ghastly sight of dying natives in the grove; or again, when Marlow criticises the administration that gives these black men three nine-inch long brass-wire pieces a week as their wages, which fail to buy them anything. He dissuades them from the habit of cannibalism and does not allow them to eat each other in his presence.

Throughout the novella, Marlow pronounces the kinship between the howling, screaming Congolese and the rest of humanity, climaxed by the look given him by the dying negro helmsman, a look creating a "subtle bond" between them. He considers his helmsman as a valuable human being like Kurtz. In the end, Marlow returns to Europe and seals his commitment to Kurtz by lying to his fiancée. She wants to know what his last words were, and it seems to Marlow too dark altogether to tell her the truth. He tells her instead what she wants to hear, that the last word Kurtz uttered was her name. This lie is an act of benevolent and idealistic motivation. The truth would only have plunged her into needless disillusionment and pain.

Marlow as Projection of Conrad

There is plenty of internal evidence of the identity of Conrad and Marlow. Conrad's biographers acknowledge the point, and Conrad insists upon it in his Author's Note: "Youth is a feat of memory...a record of experience...Heart of Darkness is experience, too: but it is experience pushed a little (and only very little) beyond the actual facts of the case...". Clearly, Conrad wished to take responsibility for the meditative and didactic components of Marlow's narratives, as well as their factual content. One would expect the meditating voice projected in the fiction to be the meditative projection of Conrad himself. A variety of evidence confirms this expectation: Marlow's language and opinions tally so closely with Conrad's as to suggest a deliberate projection of the author into his character. Marlow's chaffing humor" is undoubtedly Conrad's. Marlow becomes less a person than an intellectual voice.

His Englishness

The switchboard through which the comment passes is Marlow. Whatever his usefulness to the author in the four tales in which he appears as narrator, Marlow is of particular value to Conrad as a bridge to England, or more exactly to the quality of being English to Englishness. The five years from 1895 to 1900, from *Almayer's Folly to Lord Jim*, are the period of Conrad's first and most serious attempt to establish himself in England, root simply as a welcome foreigner but as a man who could take root from within. Marlow is Conrad's most sustained effort in getting inside an English skin. He is not Conrad in toto; he is Conrad in his English manifestation, the Pole striving to be a Briton.

Aside from the fact that he is English and an officer in the British merchant marine, that he bears an English name and speaks the language idiomatically, Marlow embodies the ideas and functions which, Conrad associates with the genius of his adopted country. He allies with Kurtz because he can talk to him in English. He refuses to deliver any document to the office of the trading company because he does not want to expose the atrocities perpetrated by imperialism on the African people. He hands over the famous report to the journalist for publication after tearing off the foot-note "Exterminate all the brutes." He does not do or say anything against the English people or society.

Like a true Englishman, he assumes a middle-of-the-road position on everything and seeks to mediate between the extremes; in this, he embodies the British spirit of compromise. He mediates between the illusioned, sentimental innocence of Kurtz's Intended and the complex Satanism of Kurtz himself, between the light of civilisation and the darkness of primitivism, between colonialising Europe and exploiting Africa. In *Lord Jim*, he seeks to restore Jim to balance between his warring selves. He is, throughout, the supreme compromiser, the moderator of the show who yet does not renounce his own views; his role as a technician is constantly reinforced and humanised by his private apparatus of moral opinion and amateur philosophising.

A Preserver and not a Destroyer

Marlow seeks to save. He saves Jim, saves himself by telling the necessary lie to Kurtz's fiancée, saves Flora de Barral from committing suicide, saves the crew in the lifeboat after the sinking of the *Judea.* When he is not saving, he is recording, totaling up moral accounts, building a system of communications strong enough to withstand the malignant and hostile disorders that afflict men. He strives to preserve not only himself but those around him, those within reach. His exertions remain unceasing, a supreme display of virtuoso energy, in itself a mark of an informing, life-producing vitality. He expresses his disgust over the dying and starving black African. He saves the dead body of his helmsman from being eaten away by his fellow men. He saves Kurtz from performing another "unspeakable rite" of sacrificing a young man at his altar; he saves Kurtz's reputation in Europe; he tells a lie to his Intended to keep her faith in her lover intact. He is the conscience of the community. Marlow delivers his moral report, plays the role of an honest broker, and invokes the Whiteman's burden, discharging, in short, the historical functions of the Englishman.

Conclusion

Marlow is a detective of the human soul in *Heart of Darkness.* In this novella, he follows clues toward solving the mystery of Kurtz. He suffers a mental crisis through his encounter with Kurtz. The two Marlows – one in *Lord Jim* and the other in *Heart of Darkness* are also dissimilar in certain ways. It is the nature of Conrad's narrators to become only what the meanings of the novels require of them. They have, most crucially, quite different moral standards in certain points. Although Marlow's prove willing to lie for, or at least excuse, the moral failings of their mysterious "partners," the object of Jim's Marlow is to reveal his subject's greatness," whereas Kurtz's Marlow ultimately strives to conceal it. The Marlow of *Lord Jim* believes that even dangerous knowledge is worthy of public examination, whereas 'the Marlow of *Heart of Darkness* believes the contrary: that dangerous knowledge must be suppressed.

We must conclude that, Marlow does recount events in *Heart of Darkness* chronologically. He acts as a kind of chorus, as in Greek tragedy. But he has other uses, too, and they result from Conrad's wish to distance himself from the experience behind the tale. Conrad looks at events through the eyes of Marlow, much older and wiser, who can recapture the flavour of past incidents and yet avoid sentimentality. His function is to convey the horror of the seductive power of the jungle and its natives.

References

Ambrosini, Richard, *Conrad's Fiction as Critical Discourse.* Cambridge Univ. Press. 1991. Print.

Andreach, Robert J., *The Slain and Resurrected God: Conrad, Ford, and the Christian Myth.* New York: New York University Press. 1970. Print.

Bancroft, William W., *Joseph Conrad: His Philosophy of Life.* Philadelphia: Stratford Co. 1930. Print.

Goddard Lisa, *Conrad and the Critics: Responses to Heart of Darkness,* published on July 17, 2012. https://landing.athabascau.ca/blog/view/136720/conrad-and-the-critics-responses-to-heart-of-darkness [Accessed on 18 December 2021]

Guerard, Albert J., *Conrad the Novelist.* Cambridge Harvard University Press, c.1958. Print.

Johnson, Cynthia Brantley, *Heart of Darkness and the Secret Sharer (Enriched Classic).* New York: Simon & Schuster, Inc. Papaerbacks, 2009. Print.

Kipling Rudyard, "The White Man's Burden: The United States & the Philippine Islands, 1899." *Rudyard Kipling's Verse: Definitive Edition, Garden* City, New York: Doubleday, 1929.

Palmer, John A. *Joseph Conrad's Fiction A Study in Literary Growth.* New York: Cornell University Press; First Edition (January 1, 1968). Print.

Web Sources:

https://studylib.net/doc/25358721/heart-of-darkness-assignment-2020

https://literatureessaysamples.com/heart-of-darkness-metaphorical-or-physical-journey/

https://www.academia.edu/5057756/Heart_of_Darknessheart_of_darkness

CHAPTER 16

Cognitive Perspective in Sculpting Travel Memories

Dr. Gargi Singh

Abstract

The cognitive perspective of travel memories presented in the current article explores perspectives of travel experiences on human cognition and memory. Though the thoughts in the paper are driven by and large by positive emotions and construction of memories, it's imperative to understand that it is a subjective experience of an individual that has been described in relation to the significance of travel, memories created and recalled. Memory is a worth exploring term in relation to human thinking. The current article describes in detail the cognitive aspects of sculpting travel related memories. Long-term memory and predominantly the role of episodic memory and its functional aspects in retrieving travel memories from experiences. The details that are covered while retrieving and recalling hold a great importance while drawing relation of role of episodic memory and travel. Scope of the article draws connections between dominant ways in which a travel experience is retrieved and recalled by a traveller. The insights in this article are inspired by personal experiences wherein an attempt has been made to draw connections with the social aspects as stimulants to thinking and generating memories. The perspective through which independent travel with purpose or for the sake of enjoyment has also been an aspect explored in the article.

Introduction

Travel as defined by Cambridge dictionary means "to make a journey, usually over a long distance". Born and brought up in a small town of Rajasthan and that too in a city that had been full of travellers as it had been the religious spot of people from different religious communities. I clearly remember my family actively involved as a host to many relatives who visited the pious city once in a year. Being surrounded by an environment where my relatives visit meant another tour for us to explore the city again and an escape from the academic routines. Amidst this social exchange how I turned seven, and in search of my memories this figure became very striking, as this was the time, I literally made the verb 'travel', happen in my life. The question that arises at this point is will I be searching the action points of my travel through cognitive abilities of thinking and recall. Next is the point, does my cognition really support the memories I hold for my travel experiences, or is it a rocket science that will make me struggle to reach my brain space. Also, at this moment when I want to travel my memories related to my first ever travel would a social support system be quintessential. Hence if my brain is the one that is responsible to store all these memories, it is essential to understand the cognitive perspective and the types of memories that could support the travel memories and its relation to recall.

A theoretical Perspective – Cognitive structure and Memory

Memory is today defined in psychology as the faculty of encoding, storing, and retrieving information (Squire, 2009). Memory is a mental process by which information is encoded, stored and retrieved (Atkinson and Shiffrin, 1968) although memory may also refer to the information itself, the memory that we recall and remember (Winstanley, 2006). Cognitive psychology recognises two major types of memory having different capability and capacity. Short-term memory (working memory) is able to store information for certain period of time but with limited capacity, whereas long-term memory has a large capacity and contains memories of experiences and information that have accumulated over a life-time. Two types of long-term memory are distinguished: semantic and episodic memory (Pearce and Packer, 2013; Tung et al., 2016). Semantic memory is memory of general knowledge about the world (Tung et al., 2016; Braun-LaTour et al., 2006), whereas episodic memory refers to specific memories such as personal experience (Pearce and Packer, 2013) and events (Braun-LaTour et al., 2006). Autobiographical memory is a subset of episodic memory (Conway and Pleydell-Pearce, 2000; Tung et al., 2016) and defined as recollected events that belong to the person's past (Rubin, 2005; Pearce and Packer, 2013; Tung and Ritchie, 2011a). The spreading activation model (Collins and Loftus, 1975) describes how an entire network of ideas (schema) is searched to retrieve specific information from our memory. I would first elaborate on the long term memory in order to connect it further with travel memories.

Long Term Memory

LTM or the long-term memory is the relatively permanent and limitless storehouse of the memory system. It constitutes each person's knowledge of the world. Materials in the long-term memory helps one solve problems, manipulate abstract symbols and to reason. This further helps in creativity. The knowledge in our LTM is stored in an orderly and organised manner and different cues help us to recall exactly what we want to recall.

a) Procedural memory/non declarative/implicit memory:

It is also known as implicit memory. Procedural memory is the knowledge of learning by doing. It is the storehouse for our various skills. It is the way of remembering of how things are done/how a task is performed. E.g. Bicycle riding, typing, baking a cake (without thinking, consciously these are done mechanically)

b) Declarative memory /explicit memory:

It is also known as explicit memory. It consists of all the information which can be easily put into words. In other words, it consists of all the "what" aspects of information. Declarative memory can further be divided into two types:

Episodic Memory

The concept of episodic memory, according to Tulving (1983, 2002), refers to a declarative memory that contains information specific to the time and place of acquisition (what laypeople may call an autobiographical episode), as distinguished from semantic memory, which is concerned with knowledge not tied to its context of acquisition. It stores memories of your personal experiences such as first day of school, birthdays etc. Thus, memory for specific experiences of personal nature refer to episodic memory. It consists of content rich in emotional tone.

Semantic Memory

It refers to abstract knowledge. It is the storehouse of all the factual knowledge about the world and also consists of word meaning, rules of grammar etc. It is an organised knowledge about the world including the verbal world and how they are used. E.g.: The information: What is the capital of the USA will be stored here.

My first Travel – Recall from the Declarative or explicit memory

Coming back to my point of the first travel that I did and where should I get the information about it will now be answered by the declarative or the explicit memory. As my first travel is my personal experience and as it was the first travel that I did it has a lot of emotionally charged connections. So, for my first travel which ways back when I was 7-year-old was a train journey that I did in a steam engine run train and that too we were assigned by a special compartment that was an individual compartment that was allotted to my family which included my mother, elder sister and a younger brother. This was an earned privilege we received as our father served in the Indian railways. The particular travel details got stored in the explicit memory. It included the spacious compartment which just had four of us and another family. The people who accompanied us in the super luxurious compartment were three in number. The most striking part of the travel was that I remember the families' cultural connections and even the community they belonged too. The most amazing part of this travel memory was the activities that we all did, wherein for the first 5 minutes we were strangers and in the 10th minute we were friends. It started with the mothers talks amongst and then I and my two siblings were the closest to the two big brothers who belonged to the other family. The beauty of the travel was that the 18 hours journey which started with strangers concluded with a relationship of friendship bond, developed in mere 17 hours and 55 minutes. The take aways of this journey had been, two things that I clearly remember – the game of Ludo that I saw for the first time with them and an English song that I learnt on the journey. This song is now sung by my son and daughter too. I could picture this long-ago scene perfectly as the episodic memory allowed me to mentally time-travel back to an episode of my life and relive it in vivid details. I also used episodic memory to remember the names and number of people and even the activities we did together. So, the episodic memory enables one to remember to take a detour because there is construction along our usual route. In fact, most of the time when we speak about "memory," we are referring to episodic memory, which involves several parts of the brain. Even researches support that a memory qualifies as an episodic memory, if at the time of retrieval; it covers details of the event and of the place in which it occurred accompanied by auto noetic consciousness that enables re-experiencing [James 1950, p. 658; Tulving 1983, 2002; see Rubin & Umanath 2015 for a critique and alternative].

The hippocampus is crucial for episodic memory. It is always at work as it is recording thoughts, feelings, perceptions, and sensations that arise from other regions of the brain. One part of the hippocampus binds these desperate aspects of experience into a coherent whole. Another part tags it with an index that will allow the memory to be retrieved minutes, hours, days or years later. Hence my first travel memory is still so fresh and sequentially aligned as the Hippocampus supported its existence.

However, the big question is related to the extensive details of the recalled episode, wherein I could remember the details of the face of people, the look of the game, the song and much more. Here comes the role of two hippocampi, frontal lobes and the parietal lobes, one on each side. The left-brain system is specialised for words and language. The right-brain system is particularly good at remembering non-linguistic information including images, body language, and tone of voice. So, when you recall a conversation with your friend, your left hippocampus remembers the words that were spoken, and your right hippocampus remembers how they were spoken, your friend's face, and the emotion conveyed.

Social Cognitive Perspective to Travel Memories

As per psychology the human behaviour can be categorised as cognitive, affective and conative. Getting back to my first travel experience it was a journey that satisfied my affective or the emotional behaviour the most and it can be considered as a happy memory. Further to research evidences, one of the most striking findings in recent years points to the large overlap in processes and structures involved in retrieving episodic memories, imagining future personal events, and constructing scenes, thereby propelling the Hippocampus into domains it had not occupied previously (Addis & Schacter 2011, Buckner 2010, Maguire & Mullally 2013, Schacter et al. 2012, Viard et al. 2012). Research done by Schacter and Addis 2007 considers the relation between past and future events from the perspective of the constructive episodic simulation hypothesis, which holds that episodic simulation of future events requires a memory system that allows the flexible recombination of details from past events into novel scenarios. Waytz et al. (2015) demonstrated that mental simulations, especially those that are detailed and vivid, positively contribute to the experience of meaning in life. The participants of this research reported evidence that self-reported meaning in life is positively correlated with neural activation in the medial temporal lobes subsystem of the 'default mode network.' The medial temporal lobes are notably associated with vivid and detailed episodic simulations (Addis, Cheng, Roberts, & Schacter, 2011; for a review, Szpunar, 2010), suggesting that the vividness of simulations may be especially important to a sense of meaning in life. Though all these are cognitive perspectives, however one can relate it so well when memories of travel are retrieved and if it was satisfactory for an individual, it facilitates more travel aspirations through which a person seems to be satisfied and even aspires to travel more for personal well-being.

Memories of Independent Travel

Official Travel with Purpose

Connecting to my own travel diaries, since my first travel experience that includes the yearly travels with my family these memories were fixed destinations to meet relatives staying in Gujarat, Uttar Pradesh or Punjab, until I reached a stage of independent travel. Independent travel brings our attention to vacations. Thinking about vacations may stimulate fantasy (Rubenstein, 1980), and emotions that play an important role in shaping vacation destination choices (Decrop and Snelders, 2004). Pleasurable vacation experiences are sought for fun, amusement, fantasy and sensory stimulation (Babin et al., 1994; Holbrook, 2006). However my independent travel and destination was official and again was positive and pleasurable. It was to a beautiful city of Gujarat i.e. Vadodara where I went for my higher studies. The memories I have of going to this place all by my own and then exploring the university space and courses was a journey altogether. It again was a social experience with people and places that still evoke Positive and pleasurable emotions and feelings. These two components are important experiences for travel destinations (Tung and Ritchie, 2011a). Essentially I am talking about this memory from affect, emotion or mood point of view. First I will differentiate the terms affect, emotions and mood, as often they are inconsistently used in literature (Ma et al., 2013, p. 19; Li et al., 2015;

Bagozzi et al., 1999). Affect is commonly viewed as an umbrella term for specific mental processes, such as emotions, moods and attitudes (Bagozzi et al., 1999; Ma et al., 2013, p. 21), whereas mood state is allocated from any particular object or event and refers to an affective state with a low level of intensity (Huang et al., 2012). Emotions may result in intense feelings and be associated with a specific factor, such as event or person (Li et al., 2015). I still get in an emotional state of happiness when I recall my experiences at Vadodara. The 'garba' nights and the culturally aligned city, its loving people and the youth spirit they all seemed to be a perfect combination to suit my social cognitive structure of adapting the place and even having positive feeling about the place and people. There is a significant literature on memory and emotions in cognitive psychology which focuses on topics such as memory accuracy in emotional recall (Thomas, 1990). Hence even in today's context the placed, food, people and the destinations in Vadodara appear crystal clear to me.

Memories of Independent Travel – Vacation

My independent travels progressively extended and I started travelling for the purpose of pleasure and even to take breaks. I travelled to multiple destinations, but one destination that took place in my long episodic memory was Puducherry. Research evidences suggest that holidays foster hedonic behaviour (Williams, 2006), they are basically pleasurable (Floyd, 1997; Gnoth, 1997; Goossens, 2000) and usually elicit positive emotions (Gretzel et al., 2006; Li et al., 2014). Holidays are memorable, and emotions influence this memorability (Larsen and Jenssen, 2004; Wirtz et al., 2003). I can hold it true for Pondicherry as it is a heaven on earth, the band stand just near the sea. Exploring the city on cycle and breathing clean air that touches your skin and hair with flavours of purity. This feeling matches to the research evidence that experience must be personally relevant, novel and surprising (Poulsson and Kale, 2004). The unusual or distinctive events experienced on a vacation are more likely to elicit higher levels of positive arousal and are therefore more likely to be remembered (Kim, 2010). Hence the social cognitive perspective engages a person in a travel experience through a process of thinking. The experiences become stimulations that generate a response to the destinations, food, clothing and the social life of the place one travels to. Perspectives are built and future choices are made to choose the destinations of travel. With every destination chosen and visited a memory is formed linked with a retrieval and recall value.

Conclusion

Overall, my learning while exploring the cognitive aspects of travel memories indicates a vast area of social cognition that could have been considered while elaborating the perspective. The role of social stimulus like cultural exchange, food, acceptance and safety holds a great impact on the experiences and also on the recall factor. Also, these social indicators impact the thinking of people to choose the destinations and also decide the frequency of travel whether independently or in groups. Hence according to my perspective, travel destination, our cognition and its connections with the felt emotions and feelings holds a great importance in sculpting our travel memories.

References

Squire, L. R. "Memory and brain systems": 1969-2009. *J. Neuroscience.* (2009). 29, 12711-12716. doi: 10.1523/jneurosci.3575-09.2009

Tulving E. *Elements of Episodic Memory.* Oxford, UK: Clarendon; 1983. [Google Scholar]

Tulving E. "Episodic memory: from mind to brain". *Annual Review Psychology.* 2002; 53:1-25. [PubMed] [Google Scholar]

James W. "*Principles of Psychology*". Vol. 1. New York: Dover; 1950 (1890). [Google Scholar]

Tulving E. "*Elements of Episodic Memory*". Oxford, UK: Clarendon; 1983. [Google Scholar]

Tulving E. "Episodic memory: from mind to brain". *Annual Review Psychology.* 2002; 53:1-25. [PubMed]

Rubin DC, Umanath S Event memory: "A theory of memory for laboratory, autobiographical, and fictional events". *Psychology Review.* 2015 Jan; 122(1):1-23.[PubMed] [Ref list]

Addis DR, Schacter DL. "The hippocampus and imagining the future: Where do we stand? Front Human Neuroscience". 2011; 5:173. [PMC free article] [PubMed] [Google Scholar]

Buckner RL. "The role of the hippocampus in prediction and imagination". *Annual Review Psychology.* 2010; 61:27-48

Maguire, E. A., & Mullally, S. L. (2013). "The hippocampus: A manifesto for change". *Journal of Experimental Psychology: General,* 142(4), 1180-1189. http://dx.doi.org/10.1037/a0033650

Schacter DL, Addis DR, Hassabis D, Martin VC, Spreng RN, Szpunar KK. "The future of memory: remembering, imagining, and the brain". *Neuron.* 2012; 76:677-94

Schacter, D. L., & Addis, D. R. (2007). "The cognitive neuroscience of constructive memory: remembering the past and imagining the future". *Philosophical Transactions of the Royal Society of London B: Biological Sciences*, 362(1481), 773-786.

Viard A, Desgranges B, Eustache F, Piolino P." Factors affecting medial temporal lobe engagement for past and future episodic events: an ALE meta-analysis of neuroimaging studies". *Brain Cognition.* 2012; 80:111-25.

Addis, D. R., Cheng, T., Roberts, R. P., & Schacter, D. L... "Hippocampal contributions to the episodic simulation of specific and general future events". Hippocampus, (2011) 21, 1045-1052. doi:10.1002/hipo.20870

Waytz, A., Hershfield, H. E., & Tamir, D. I. (2015). "Mental simulation and meaning in life". *Journal of Personality and Social Psychology*, 108, 336-355. doi:10.1037/a0038322

Liubov Skavronskaya, Noel Scott, Brent Moyle, Dung Le, ArghavanHadinejad, Rui Zhang, Sarah Gardiner, Alexandra Coghlan, Aishath Shakeela, (2017) "Cognitive psychology and tourism research: state of the art", *Tourism Review*, Vol. 72 Issue: 2, pp.221-237,

Atkinson, R.C. and Shiffrin, R.M. (1968), "Human memory: a proposed system and its control processes", *Psychology of Learning and Motivation*, Vol. 2, pp. 89-195.

Winstanley, J. (2006), *Key Concepts in Psychology*, Palgrave Macmillian, Basingstoke.

Pearce, P.L. and Packer, J. (2013), "Minds on the move: new links from psychology to tourism", *Annals of Tourism Research*, Vol. 40 No. 1, pp. 386-411.

Conway, M.A. and Pleydell-Pearce, C.W. (2000), "The construction of autobiographical memories in the self-memory system", *Psychological Review*, Vol. 107 No. 2, p. 261.

Floyd, M.F. (1997), "Pleasure, arousal, and dominance: exploring affective determinants of recreation satisfaction", *Leisure Sciences*, Vol. 19 No. 2, pp. 83-96.

Williams, A. (2006), "Tourism and hospitality marketing: fantasy, feeling and fun", *International Journal of Contemporary Hospitality Management*, Vol. 18 No. 6, pp. 482-495

Gretzel, U., Fesenmaier, D.R., Formica, S. and O'Leary, J.T. (2006), "Searching for the future: challenges faced by destination marketing organizations", *Journal of Travel Research,* Vol. 45 No. 2, pp. 116-126.

Poulsson, S.H.G. and Kale, S.H. (2004), "The experience economy and commercial experiences", Marketing Review, Vol. 4 No. 3, pp. 267-277.

Kim, J.H. (2010), "Determining the factors affecting the memorable nature of travel experiences", *Journal of Travel & Tourism Marketing*, Vol. 27 No. 8, pp. 780-796.

CHAPTER 17

Illusion versus Reality in *An Area of Darkness* by V. S. Naipaul

Dr. Yashoda Verma

Abstract

Diaspora novels have created a new literary craze by painting life experiences in international colors. The novel, *An Area of Darkness* (1964) published by V. S. Naipaul depicts the diasporic dimensions of Naipaul's life experiences. *An Area of Darkness* is a novel in which Naipaul portrays India as a "dark area." He believes that such countries are places where people are subjected to humiliation and oppression, where there are no human rights and no gender equality. It's an emotional travelogue published in 1964 during his first trip to India. Naipaul's ironic perspective in India alludes to society's decay. He primarily serves as a representative of western beliefs and world views in An Area of Darkness and stands in contrast to the rest of Indian civilisation. Naipaul writes about his travels, which took him to India, Pakistan, Malaysia, Indonesia, the Ivory Coast, Iran, Argentina, and Uruguay, among other places. The novel's central themes are alienation and solitude. It chronicles his failed attempt to settle in India. In this novel, Naipaul began a difficult battle with the culture that had fostered him since his childhood and had identified him as a kind of resident alien in the west.

Keywords: Postcolonial, Society, life experience, Identity crisis, diaspora, Assertion.

V. S. Naipaul's novel, *An Area of Darkness* published in 1964 is a travelogue about Naipaul's trip through India in the early 1960s. It was the first book in Naipaul's acclaimed trilogy, which also included *India: A Wounded Civilisation* (1977) and *India: A Million Mutinies Now* (1990). It is the most emotional and subjective of the books. It tells of his first trip to his forefathers' homeland. It is full of descriptions of India's terrible poverty. India, according to Naipaul, is "the poorest country in the world." According to Naipaul, Indians defecate everywhere yet refuse to acknowledge it. He examines the reasons why he believes poverty is so prevalent in India in a very logical manner. At one point, he talks of how the "split of the brain from body labour has created the story emphasises the tumultuous connection". The current research provides a new perspective on V S Naipaul, not just as a writer but also as a visionary thinker. "A travel book written by an author with little personality is likely to be boring; a travel book written by an author with pronounced personality (such as Mr. Naipaul) is likely to tell us more about the author than the country" (Riley, 1975, p.371). Naipaul's predicament is depicted in the first scene of *An Area of Darkness*. A Travelers Prelude is an interlude rather than a prelude. When Naipaul arrives at the Bombay docks during the early 1960s prohibition era, he discovers at customs that the bottles of liquor he brought with him from Alexandria have been confiscated. Naipaul encounters bureaucratic difficulties while attempting to recover them at Bombay's New Custom House. The country of India is more visible in objects than in people. The things and people produced by India, according to Naipaul, are featureless and dark. Even though his grandfather had left India, he did not forget Indian customs and manners. In fact, when he built his house in Trinidad, he ignored every colonial-style design he came across. Nothing enticed or compelled him to participate in any activity except his own village in India. Because the settlers had preferences in everything, life was simple in Trinidad. They learned to do their jobs without the help of sweepers, weavers, dyers, brass workers, or string bed makers. Masons, carpenters, and cobblers, on the other hand, were present. The sight of Indian filth terrified Naipaul. Animals are fed from plates that have been used by humans. The children exchanged a variety of sweets. Women drank from the same ladles they used to stir their pots. Naipaul's imaginative approach to caste differences and religious rituals is emphasised, "I remained unhappy. Being an unorthodox hotel, we attracted the orthodox. There had been the Brahmin family, the first of many, who had insisted on cooking for themselves. They shelled peas, sifted rice, and cut carrots in the doorway of their room; they cooked in the broom cupboard below the steps and washed their pots and pans at the garden tap; they turned part of the new turf to mud. Others threw their rubbish on the lawn; others spread their washing on the lawn. And I believed that the idyll was at an end when Aziz announced one day, with a well-managed mixture of enthusiasm and condolence that twenty orthodox Indians were coming to the hotel for four days. Some would sleep in the dining room; we would eat in the sitting room. I was beyond condolence. Aziz recognised this and offered none. We waited. Aziz became morose, almost offended, in our presence. But the twenty did not turn up, and then for a day or two Aziz looked genuinely offended." (*An Area of Darkness*, 111)

Similarly, the projection of caste in the novel was designed to cause harm and division in India, but it had no effect on Trinidadian culture. He despised the sight of Indians with caste stains on their hands. Naipaul was uninterested in Hinduism or its religious practices. He despised the new baby thread ceremony. West Indian writers, particularly George Lamming, chastised Naipaul for not paying enough attention to non-Indian groups in his works. Naipaul's private world was shrinking and weakening as he moved away from the featureless area of darkness that was India. It's easy to sympathize with Naipaul's distress over the deterioration of old customs. The ancient order and established world were respected by the Indians. Naipaul despised tradition, and he was outraged when he learned that the Diwali festival in Bombay was celebrated with candles and electric bulbs. However, people of Indian origin in Trinidad have been using rustic clay lamps. The Naipaul travelogues portray or explain the religious landscape of various groups throughout South Asia, not just in India. Paul White states, "it must be noted that amongst all the literature of migration the highest proportion deals in some way with ideas of return, whether actualised or remaining imaginary." (Writing across Worlds: Literature and Migration, p. 14). His point of view is critical because he observes a gap between appearance and reality in religious orientations, as well as a lot of cultural projection or ethnocentric impact. People are unsympathetic and insensitive to one another because they live in the illusion of religious manifestations, he says in his speech; however, Naipaul presents an integrative view of human liberation from these religious forces, and he attempts to explore religion and myths from this perspective. "It is well that Indians are unable to look at their country directly, for the distress they would see would drive them mad. And it is well that they have no sense of history, for how then would they be able to continue to squat amid their ruins, and which Indian would be able to read the history of his country for the last thousand years without anger and pain? It is better to retreat into fantasy and fatalism, to trust to the stars in which the fortunes of all are written" (Naipaul, 1964) His excursions are symbolic of the mystic notion of initiation or transformation. They develop an archetype psychic sentiment who wishes to construct an allegorical story through his inner vision by examining the waking vision of the stations he travels through. These travelogues could be considered narratives of an expatriate argumentative Indian who, while searching for his identity, encounters cultural practices in India, Pakistan, and Iran that are coincidentally associated in defining their origin, history, religion, and identity building realities. This instils in the reader a new sense of awareness and maturity. His sensitive records provide an empirical perspective for moral and social inquiry, demystifying moral and social inquiry elements. In his introduction to Naipaul's recent collection of essays, appropriately titled "The Writer and the World", Pankaj Mishra writes, "It is difficult to think of one writer so fundamentally exilic, carrying so many clashing fading worlds inside him." What's more remarkable is Naipaul's acute sense of lost glory and contentment [and here I must interject and ask, "What glory, what contentment?"] And who is it? Naipaul's, or the worlds he chooses to explore?], his anguished perception of deception and tragedy – [again, I must interrupt and remind you that Naipaul states, 'The world is what it is' – our inherited tragedy as a species] – things inextricably linked to his background and experience – coexist with an attitude of acceptance and optimism, with a firm belief in human striving and perfectibility".

According to Naipaul, Indians were not treated as human beings, even by other Indians. Everyone is conceited and envious of others. They, too, showed a lack of regard for their profession. Rather than training their children in their own profession, they are looking for other opportunities for their children. According to Naipaul, the Hindu holy book, *Bhagavat Geeta* is ineffective because it has created a psychological barrier in people's minds that leads to frustration. Despite his political success, Mahatma Gandhi was a failed reformer, according to Naipaul. In India, all that remains of Gandhi is his name and the veneration of his image. Gandhi's message is lost as he becomes a God. An Area of Darkness, on the other hand, is adept at concealing the traces of its existence and its own recognition. "India depicted in Naipaul's *An Area of Darkness* is a country in a spectacular state of decay. Its people have been "degraded" and "stupefied," its religions have become "outdated," and its buildings, if not already in ruins, "hint at the imminence of their own destruction" (Naipaul, 1964, p. 216). Naipaul has not been enchanted by India. Even though he used to avoid it, it remained a dark place.

His one-year journey did not teach him acceptance; instead, he learned his alienation from India. Naipaul was content to be a colonial, with no history or ancestors. Naipaul paints a picture of India's railways. What we can deduct from this account is that Naipaul wants to convey his deliberate orientation to a situation in which religion dominates in social and cultural terms, but business, whether local, national, or international, does not transcend religion, but rather flowering sensibility and poignant human emotional responses take precedence over religious instincts. As a result, his literary travelogues can build a vogue against the political and social injustices resulting from religion's supremacy, notably in pre-and post-colonial South Asian nations. His ambivalence about national feelings and belonging to a specific country is a fundamental predisposition for his perception of India. Despite growing up in Trinidad's Hindu community, he is estranged from his grandfather's homeland. The main difference between Indians in Trinidad and Indians in India was the vast geographical distance between them. Over nearly a century of emigration, the gap between those in Trinidad and those in India widened, and two distinct cultures emerged as a result. The author's imagined India bears no resemblance to the real India. "My train was due to leave in about two hours; the coaches were waiting. I changed my third-class ticket for a first-class one, picked my way down dim platforms, past the bodies of dogs and men, past third-class carriage which was already hot. The conductor opened the door of my compartment and I climbed it. I bolted the door, pulled down all the blinds, trying to shut out the howls of dogs, shuttling out intrudes all those staring faces and skeletal bodies. I put on no lights. I required darkness (Naipaul, 1964, p. 239)". Naipaul depicts the state of the Eastern world, which includes not only India but also Africa. The writer, who has visited London, finds the Indian scenario intolerable. At the outset, he has a bad encounter at the customs in Bombay. Seeing the officials' mismanagement irritates him greatly. He goes to the New Customs office twice to obtain a liquor permit. In India, he observes people's attitudes toward work, where they place a higher value on their dignity than on their ability to accomplish a task. When he asked a clerk at the Customs office to get him a glass of water, he was ignored, which he found insulting. "A clerk was a clerk; a messenger was a messenger," he recalls afterward (Naipaul, 15). Naipaul portrays two characters in "A Resting Place for Imagination," he communicates his image of India, which portrays him in the minds of the people as an estranged man from India. Individuals are less visible in India than objects are. Naipaul sees India's products, as well as its people, as featureless and black. Even though his grandfather had left India, he did not forget Indian customs and etiquette. In fact, he avoided every colonial design he could find in Trinidad when constructing his mansion. Nothing lured or drove him to participate in any activity more than his home village in India. Life was simple in Trinidad since the settlers had first dibs on everything. The critic Dhawan (2000) illustrates, "In *An Area of Darkness*, obviously, Naipaul has become a victim of the dilemma…why to use the western criteria in determining India to be an area of light or darkness… I wish Naipaul could identify himself with the dirt, squalor, and poverty of India (Dhawan, 2000, p. 143)." "It was a journey that ought not to have been made; it had broken my life into two" (Naipaul, 1964, p.215).

An Area of Darkness is Naipaul's sincere attempt to grapple with issues of identity. The acute perception of his own rootlessness and displacement shaped Naipaul's creative talent. As a diaspora writer, Naipaul's approach is very limited. His writing is tainted by feelings of alienation and isolation from India. Exile and alienation are prevalent themes in twentieth-century literature about exile. To Naipaul, the India he associated with the people and things around him was devoid of character. The critic, Rohler points out that "the position of ironist in colonial society is indeed a delicate one. The early Naipaul is at times the irresponsible ironist. Satire is the sensitive measures of a society's departure from the norm inherent in itself……. this explains the mixture of farce and social consciousness which occurs on the two early novels".

An Area of Darkness is a genuine attempt in which Naipaul does not try to appear larger than he is, and the underlying self-portrait is unflattering. His nerves are always on edge, and he appears to be on the defensive all the time. His reactions are frequently irrational, culminating in self-criticism. His detractors have spoken of his displacement, of being born a foreigner, a citizen of an exclusive community on a colonised island with no natural home other than India, where he frequently returns, only to be reminded of his distance from his roots. He has left an almost confessional record of his cultural disinheritance and its personal implications in An Area of Darkness. His visit to India confirms his fears and forebodings that the land of his ancestors is still in the grip of darkness. His journey through his forefather's diverse homeland only confirms his alienation from India. He is satisfied to be a colonial without a past, without ancestors.' This is amply demonstrated by An Area of Darkness. The blend of real and imagined in this and other travel texts varies depending on Naipaul's emotions and mood at the time of writing. This is more akin to the act of writing a poem or a novel that expresses the writer's disposition and proclivity than the factual and conspicuously observable phenomena expected of a travelogue.

References

Bhabha, Homi. *The Location of Culture.* London: Routledge, 1994.

Boehmer, Elleke. *Colonial and Postcolonial Literature: Migrant Metaphors.* Oxford UP, 1995.

Brubaker, Rogers. "The 'diaspora' diaspora" (PDF). Ethnic and Racial Studies". 28 (1): 1-19. doi:10.1080/0141987042000289997. S2CID 17914353, 2005.Retrieved 22 February 2011.

Clingman, Stephen. *The Grammar of Identity: Transnational Fiction and the Nature of the Boundary.* Oxford: Oxford UP, 2009.

Cudjoe, Selwyn Reginald. *V. S. Naipaul: A Materialist Reading.* Amherst: U of Massachusetts P, 1988.

Dooley, Gillian. "A Definition of the Writing Self: The Enigma of Arrival." VS. *Naipaul: An Anthology of Recent Criticism.* Ed. Purabi Panwar. Delhi: Pencraft International, 2003. 155-7.

Jay, Paul. *Global Matters: The Transnational Turn in Literary Studies.* Ithaca: Cornell UP, 2010.

King, Bruce Alvin. *V. S. Naipaul.* Houndmills: Palgrave Macmillan, 1993.

Naipaul V.S, *An Area of Darkness.* London: Penguin Books, 1968.

.... "Prologue to an Autobiography." *Literary Occasions.* Introduction and Edited. Pankaj Mishra. New York: Alfred A. Knopf, 2003. 53-111.

Gordon Rohler, the ironic approach: the novel of V.S Naipaul, Ed: in Louis James, *the islands in between: an essay in West Indian literature.* (London Oxford University Press, 1968).

Riley, C. *Contemporary Literary Criticism.* Vol: 4. Michigan: Gale Research Inc. 1975.

Tiffin, Helen M. "Rites of Resistance: Counter-Discourse and West Indian Biography." *Journal of West Indian Literature* 3.1 (1989), pp. 28-46.

White, Paul. "Geography, Literature and Migration," *Writing across Worlds: Literature and Migration.* London: Routledge, 1995.

CHAPTER 18

Narrative of Quest for Spirituality and Emergence of Self in Yolande's *India, India*

Dr. Tanuja Yadav

Abstract

The desire to travel and visit the new places and know the culture of the other that is unknown or different from one's own place paves the way to the imagination and travel writing. The pictorial quality of the travel narrative of the 'Other' portrays the truth and liveliness of the journey. In the travel narratives, we see the 'Other' and its multiple images from the lens of the tourist or the traveler. The physical and emotional behavior of the traveler plays an important role in the narration of the travel writing or the story of the novel. This paper explores the journey of Yolande Villemaire, a Quebec writer, to India. Her sense of belonging to her roots in Quebec, Canada is expressed through her description of the people, culture, and places of India. Yolande disseminates the various images of her own country while portraying the images of India. Her description shows her perception for the east as the 'Other' but at the same time she accepts the richness of spirituality and the culture in India. The protagonist Miliana Tremblay, from Montreal, came to India in search of self through the spirituality but could not resist the difference of the east and west. She shows the lack of confidence, trust in the people from India. The dominant role of the protagonist highlights the difference and the inherent sense of superiority among the western and European travelers through the sharing of her experiences during the journey.

Keywords: Travel, Self, Experience, Spirituality, Culture, Orient

Travelogue is the transcription of the moments of the journey that are accepted and recorded in the mind of the traveler. It's true that we accept and memorise only those moments which are either exotic or different from our country, people, and places. The moments that appeals to the traveler during the journey are visible in his writing. The writing sometimes turns out into the form of the novel and the protagonist of the novel becomes the voice of the traveler. The target audience or the readers plays a vital role in the writing of the travelogue. The writer traces those experiences in the narrative that will attract the readers of that book. Thus, the presentation of the exotic other is an important part of the travel writing.

This paper deploys the concept of transnational and transcultural identity and the feeling of otherness through the novel India, India of Yolande Villemaire, a Quebec writer from Canada. This paper entails the personal experiences of Yolande during her visit to India. The attraction for the spirituality and the rich culture of India influences Yolande Villemaire to visit India. Her experience of travelling and visiting various places in India from South to Delhi and then Taj Mahal in Agra to Hawa Mahal in Rajasthan to Hyderabad motivates her to narrate her observation and her experience in the other land and the other culture particularly to the people of her country. The presence of the elements of the travelogue in the novel "India, India" focuses on the quest of the spirituality and the construction of self among the 'Others'. The touristic portrayal of the various places in India is realistic and pictorial. Her keen and minute observation of the places and the people of India highlight the differences between the two countries – India and Canada. The faith in the spirituality in India is deeply rooted in the heart of the protagonist of the novel. The confidence of the presence of God and the rich culture in India attracts the western, the other to see the 'Other'. The personal experience of the writer becomes public due to the fusion of the autobiographical and travelogue notion in the novel. It also throws light on the description of the orient, east through the lens of the West. Her sketches of the Indian people and the culture depict the western mind set up about the life and culture of the Indian society. She looks at the people of all regions; she met during her journey, not as they are at present but what she thought them to be in comparison to her own. The cliché of the Orient is already decided and treated or commented by the Occidentals. The occidents always search for the exotic elements of Orient that will attract their public to read their novel. Edward Said states,

> "[T]he Orient is not an inert fact of nature. It is not merely there, just as the Occident itself is not just there either [...] as much as the West itself, the Orient is an idea that has a history and a tradition of thought, imagery, and vocabulary that have given it reality and presence in and for the West. The two geographical entities thus support and to an extent reflect each other" (p. 4f.).

The protagonist of the novel visits India and was influenced by the guide but the deeply rooted belief of the superiority does not allow her to have faith in the Indians and especially the guide. She lacks confidence in the Indians who were on the contrary helping her in all the ways. She does not believe the people she met during her visit in India. She wants to enjoy the culture but without any faith on the people of the country. She has strong faith in the spirituality and the culture of India which was the base of her visit, but she does not trust the people who are all around her. Yolande has captured the minute details of the moments of her journey. This narration emphasises the authenticity of the description of moments in her novels. She also narrates the tradition and culture the way she perceives with the western complexity and also relate and compare them with her own place of origin. The reconstruction of self is also prevailing in the novel along with the description of the tradition, people, culture etc. of India. There are the moments where Yolande is not able to accept the things or the culture of the 'Other' due to her belonging to her land "Quebec, Canada". Being Amerindian she has emotional connections with the culture of India, but she is unable to resist herself from being stranger to the 'Other'. Her lack of trust on the Indians, especially the travel agent, Hotel receptionist, etc. during her journey emphasises the difference between the Orient and Occident, East and West, the colonised and the coloniser.

Miliana came from Montreal to visit India with all essence of spices, mixture of cardamom and pepper, perfume sticks, and also the dust and dirt. The novel traces the fear and love of the traveler, Miliana. She visited many places in all over India but she described and commented on them in her own way with her all preset mental process, thought and beliefs about the country. Yolande, while returning back to her homeland has the feeling that India is the space of illusion, where even after her long stay, something is left unrevealed and hidden. For her it is the treasure with lots more to know and to learn. She said that India is the soul of the universe. She speaks about the Dharma, le cliché of India, and speaks about her liberation from karma. Her narration of attending Kalachakra at Bodh Gaya in 2004 accentuates her faith in the spirituality that influenced her to visit India again and again.

Travel writing describes the culture, local language, religion, and local colors that are seen, observed and heard in the target places. As has been said by Elizabeth Waterson that: "a travelogue is a diary and narrative of travel, sport and adventure". According to her "it is a blend of description, anecdote and personal commentary". (Waterson 10). Yolande captured each and every minute detail of her visit since her arrival in India at the airport in Hyderabad in India with the pancarte bearing her name in the hands of the driver of car of the travelling agency to the Kalachakra in Amavarathi to Dalai Lama and then to Jawaharlal Nehru University in Delhi etc. Her lively and step by step description of her movement from one place to another make the readers visualise and enjoy the moments. The textual and visual narratives of her journey to India and in India are dominated by the presence of occidental perception. It is imperative to mention that the target readers of her novel are the public of Quebec and Canada at large. Thus, Yolande takes the pleasure in describing the exotic and unusual moments spent in India. She narrated the experiences of her journey by highlighting the cliché of India that are enjoyed and read by the occident like the spirituality, beggars, cows, yoga, and culture of India etc. Yolande described the day-to-day life images of Indians particularly the life of the Shambhala camp and the moments of prayer with Tibetans and others. Yolande has not left the chance of using the vocabulary or the language in Hindi in order to become the part of the large native group. The use of Hindi language also puts an impression of her being one of the Indians on the readers of her country. Her search for the identity among the Indians by speaking their mother language is one of the most influential elements of her writing.

Since years, people are visiting India from different parts of the world to compare and to understand the different faces of India. India with all its diversities attracts the travelers. The beautiful monuments, the stories of maharajas, holy spirits, Gods and goddesses, the tradition, people, festivals etc. all have lured the 'Others' to come and know the country in all its forms. Being the traveler, the narrator has the quest to know the unknown to her and she wants to unfold the richness of spirituality, culture and diversity of India. Yolande Villemaire, the narrator, was so deeply influenced by the culture of India that she started the first page of novel with the title "Kaalchakra". This term is taken from Vajrayana Buddhism that means "wheel of time". The Kaalchakra teachings in India were taught by Gautam Buddha. The richness of spirituality influenced her to visit India. Her narration of the various places that she visited like Delhi, Agra, and Rajasthan is very lively and authentic. She described places in Delhi like Jawarharlal Nehru University, Alliance Francaise de Delhi and Shambhala Camp. She also throws light on the streets full of beggars, lepers, small shops, stalls of plastic sandals, white scarfs, water bottles etc. The pictorial quality of the narration holds the reader and makes it lively before their eyes. Moreover, she has also explained the spices of India. The use of Hindi language serves as a catalyst in expressing the feeling of Otherness amidst the people of India. Her use of language of the country of arrival indicates her desire for being one among them. But her negative interpretation about the people in India indicates her deeply rooted feeling of superiority. At that time the rich culture and the spirituality for which she visited India does not count to her. The presence of the western mind of colonisers still lives in the perception and writing of the writers from west. The paper also posits the marginalisation of the Orient by the west and the marginalisation of the west by the orient. Yolande has portrayed the concept of caste system by imagining and inserting the concept to some of the moments during herb journey. Although the caste system of Middle Ages that is exotic for occidentals, does not have the same status at present in India, but Yolande narrates it in her novel. She knows that the narration of the caste system will attract her target audience of occident. As when Khayaal Khan, a travel agent, invited her for the tea, Yolande assumed that the driver is not invited to join them due to his caste or religion. These clichés or stereotypical approaches of Indian culture and tradition are deeply rooted in the mind of the occidentals. Hulme and Youngs (2002, p. 8) stated that, Said's "Orientalism was the first work of contemporary criticism to take travel writing as a major part of its corpus, seeing it as a body of work which offered particular insight into the operation of colonial discourses."

The name of the travel agency Dervish India Treks contacted by Miliana in Montreal has also been mentioned to indicate the authenticity. Her visit to office of Kaalchakra in Hyderabad and then informing about the distance of Shambhala camp at 2 km from Kalachakralay stress on the lively and exact portrayal of the places. This kind of narration develops the confidence of the readers for reading the novel. The descriptive writing with the use of figures authenticates the exact narration of the journey. Besides this, she preferred to use the Hindi language for some words although these words can be translated in English or French also. Yolande knows to influence the readers by developing the confidence for the exactitude of her writing. Thus the use of the language of other country reveals the deep study of the culture and tradition of the target country.

Conclusion

The journey or travelling is an important aspect for the emergence of self through the observation and evaluation with the existing self. As according to Kumar, journey is "an encounter with *heterotopoi* (other spaces) where the self – certainties of the subject are put into question" (173). For Yolande it is the heterotopic space where everything is unknown and needs to discover. The richness of the culture and spirituality moves her inner self and forces her to unveil the depth of the space. Her "self" needs to be discovered in the surrounding of the other (east).

References

Foucault, Michel, 1984. Of Other Spaces: Utopias and Heterotopias". *Architecture/Mouvement/ Continuité.*

Hulme, P. & Youngs, T., 2002. "Introduction." In: P. Hulme & T. Youngs, eds. *The Cambridge Companion to Travel Writing.* Cambridge: Cambridge University Press, pp. 1-13.

Kumar, Uday, 2002. "Seeing and Reading: The Early Malayalam Novel and Some Questions of Visibility". *Early Novels in India.* Ed. Meenakshi Mukherjee. New Delhi: Sahitya Akademi. Print.

Mills, Sarah, 1991. *Discourses of Difference: An Analysis of Women's Travel Writing and Colonialism.* London: Routledge.

Said, E., 2003. *Orientalism.* 3rd edition. London: Penguin Books Ltd.

Waterson, Elizabeth, 1956. "Travel Books," quoted in, *Literary History of Canada,* Toronto: Carl F. Klink, Vol. 362. Print.

CHAPTER 19

Seize the Day: *Zindagi Na Milegi Dobara*

Dr. Jyoti Sareen

Abstract

Literature and ideological representations of real-and-imagined spaces have a relationship. The text looks at, listens to, touches, smells, and tastes spaces and it "explores, seeks, surveys, digs into, reads, and writes a place". This paper explores the inseparable association of the story with its setting and establishes how the location complements the narrative "unfolding the interrelations between lived experience and a more abstract or unpresentable spatial net-work that subtly or directly shapes it" through analysing the movie Zindigi *Na Milegi Dobara.* It establishes that in the movie, it's the setting which propels narrative, the place and location is leading for self-discovery. The concept of travelling and introspection gets interlinked.

Keywords: Geocriticism, Spatial studies, travel, location, and self-realisation,

Dilonmein tum apnibetabiyanlekarchalraheho to

Zinda Ho Tum

Nazarmeinkhwabonki bijliyanlekarchalraheho to

Zinda Ho Tum

Hawakejhonke se azadrahanasikho

Tum ek dariyakejaiselaharonmeinbahanasikho

Har ekLamhe se tum milo kholeapnibahen

Har ek pal ek Naya samaydekhenye nigahen

Jo apniaankhonmeinhairaniyanlekarchalraheho to

Zinda Ho Tum

Dilonmein tum apnibetabiyanlekarchalraheho to

Zinda Ho Tum

> "Why do we travel, initially to lose ourselves and next to discover ourselves".
>
> Pico Iyer

Recent deconstructionist theories and particularly Foucault's discourse analysis has established that non-literary cultural forms e.g., films, advertisements, television programs, internet sites are also the text. These non-literary forms represent a significant extension of the empire of literary studies (Barry: 177), multiplicity of discourses (Barry: 176). In this paper we are moving away from the textual obsession of structuralists and post-structuralists and analysing the movie *Zindagi Na Milegi Dobara* as a text.

This paper explores the inseparable association of the story with its setting and establishes how the location complements the narrative "unfolding the interrelations between lived experience and a more abstract or unpresentable spatial net-work that subtly or directly shapes it".

Travel has been used as a trope in this movie for spiritual growth. The movie showcases a journey undertaken as a bachelor trip which turns out to be a reassessment of relations, realisation of self, negotiation with past differences and winning over fearsto seize the day. *Zindagi Na Milegi Dobara* directed by Zoya Akhtar and is written by Zoya Akhtar and Rima Kagti. It can be put under female writing phase as female director brings under scanner the destiny of male characters and main female protagonist enjoys agency, confessing her love without the fear of rejection, lives in the present and guides her tourist friends towards a real, fuller and richer life. On this journey, dark psychological recesses are also scratched to reveal the tormenting past affecting the future aspirations.

It is a road film, where story follows three childhood friends, Arjun, Kabir, and Imraan, who go on a trip to Spain, but it turns out to be a journey towards self. The film begins with Kabir proposing to Natasha. Their families are together and enjoying themselves at the engagement party where Natasha learns that Kabir is planning a three-week bachelor road trip to Spain with his school friends Imraan and Arjun. Kabir explains that the three have a long-standing pact, and that during the road trip, each of them will have to pick an adventure sport, which all three will try together. Initially, Arjun is reluctant to take part in the trip due to his work holism and obsession with money. (Arjun's ex-girlfriend left him due to this very reason).

Imraan has an additional personal agenda on the trip to find his biological father Salman Habib an artist in Spain.

The trio set off to Spain, where they plan to visit Costa Brava, Seville, and Pamplona. On the way to Costa Brava, Imraan and Kabir find it annoying that Arjun works even during the trip. Imran casually throws Arjun's phone out of their car while he was in the middle of an important call. This leads to a misunderstanding, which ends up in a violent argument. Arjun, in a fit of rage, accuses Imraan of having an affair, four years back, with Arjun's previous girlfriend (a topic which was very sensitive both to Arjun and Imraan). After getting consoled by Kabir and reaching their destination, they meet an Indian American named Laila on a beach. Imraan flirts with her and makes Arjun jealous. Kabir reveals that he has chosen deep sea diving as their first sport, and they later find that Laila is their diving instructor. Arjun, who cannot swim and is aquaphobic, receives assistance from Laila. She helps him overcome his fears and finish the sport successfully. Upon a request by Laila, they attend the La Tomatina festival held in Buñol with her and meet Nuria. Meanwhile, Natasha becomes suspicious of Kabir's involvement with Laila and crashes his bachelor party trip, much to Kabir's discomfort in front of his friends. Imraan spends time with Nuria, and Arjun with Laila. After the boys leave, Laila realises she has fallen in love with Arjun and chases them on a bike, not wanting to regret their partition if they don't meet in future.

On the way to Seville, Kabir drops Natasha at the airport, while Arjun and Imraan notice that something is wrong between her and Kabir. The trio visit Seville for skydiving, as per Arjun's choice. During the task, Imraan is forced to confront his acrophobia and hesitates to take part. However, they complete it without any obstacles. After skydiving, the three men go to a bar and get into a fight with a stranger on whom they had tried to pull a prank. They are jailed after the fight. Salman, Imraan's father, bails them out and takes them to his home. While speaking to Imraan, Salman reveals that he never wanted the responsibility of a married life with kids, while Imraan's mother did, which is why he never contacted Imraan. Imraan, heartbroken, realises how it would have felt when he had hurt Arjun four years back. He earnestly apologises to Arjun, and he readily forgives Imraan.

The trio leave for the Bull Run in Pamplona, which was Imraan's choice. When confronted by his friends, Kabir confesses to Arjun and Imraan that he is still not ready for a marriage, but could not tell this to Natasha as he did not want to hurt her. On the morning of the Bull-run, Imraan suggests they make a pact to make a promise if they survive the event. Imraan vows to publish his poetry (he was secretly a poet), Arjun vows to go to Morocco with Laila to spend the rest of his life with her, and Kabir promises to tell Natasha that he is not ready to marry her. As they complete the event, the friends gain a renewed sense of their relationships with each other, with others they know, and with themselves.

The movie ends with Imraan, Kabir, Nuria and Natasha attending the wedding of Arjun and Laila in Morocco. Kabir and Natasha did not marry, but remain friends

The movie under discussion is a new trend setter. It deviates at many points. Rather than a bachelor party with songs and dances, they plan a bachelor trip. The trope of travel has already been used for self-discovery with the aid of friend, in the movies like *Jab We Met*, What's noteworthy here that it's the setting which propels narrative, the place and location is leading for self-discovery. It is the space of the scuba diving where workaholic Arjun realises self,

1. Pighle Neelam sabehtahua yah saman
2. Neeli Neelisikhamoshiyan
3. Na kahinhai Zameen nakahinAasman
4. Sarsarati huitahniya, pattiyankahrahe hain
5. ki bus ek tum hoyahan…..
6. Sirf main hoon… Meri Saanse hain…. Meri dhadkane ….
7. Aisigehraiyaan, Aisitanhaiyan,
8. Aur main…sirfmein
9. Apne hone pe mujhkoyaqeen aa gaya

Space and Self are melting and moulting together. It was fear of death on Bull Chasethat family man Kabir confesses that his proposal was a misunderstanding on the part of Natasha. It was the setting which leads to the path of self-discovery. Kabir and Natasha are not emotionally connected to each other. It's for the family that he is getting married. Travel becomes an antidote for him. All three friends develop new skills. Space becomes a central character in this journey of realisation. It becomes a via media to understand the meaning and value of life and love.

Away from the rut of life, these new cultural settings broaden their imaginations, and they realise that it's okay to take out time for themselves. Arjun tells his friend-cum-love interest, Laila that he has plans to work till 40 and then retire. To which she asks him how he is so sure that he will live till 40. Travelling through a place becomes an opportunity for taking an inward journey. An adventure trip challenges physically, mentally, and emotionally. The concept of travelling and introspection gets interlinked. Exploring new spaces triggers 'life is in moments". Travel becomes a space for reassessment of relations, negotiation with past, coming to terms with fears and acknowledging Foucault and Rabinow that social and cultural spaces, including the body, are indeed the product of human actions, then there is the possibility of our reconstituting human spaces, and hence human being-in-the-world as well.

Travel provides them space to dive deeper into themselves. Adventure Sports have solace and peace of meditation. As a travel text, it is as inspiring as Robin Sharma's *The Monk Who Sold his Ferrari.*

Sources

Zindagi Na Milegi Dobara directed by Zoya Akhtar, Performances by Hrithik Roshan, Farhan Akhtar, Abhay Deol, Eros International, 2011.

Barry, P. *Beginning Theory: An Introduction to Literary and Cultural Theory. Manchester:* Manchester University Press, 1995.

Wegner, Philip E. *"Spatial criticism" Introducing Criticism at the 21st Century.* Ee. Julian Wolfreys, 2002

CHAPTER 20

My Trip to Maheshwar: A Memoir

Dr. Mamta Chanwaria

Abstract

A short two day trip could be of immense blissful moments, divine grace, varied experience, learning, exploring, sightseeing and of course relaxing for some leisurely hours, is what I realised after my trip to Maheshwar along with my husband. The memories still linger and innate feeling of gratitude and silence stir my heart whenever I recollect those two days. This very simple journey proved to be an enduring one and it was a journey within, as it brought before us some precious moments of peace and serenity. A combination of pilgrim and picnic, Maheshwar is a place to visit for its historical as well as mythological significance. The nature has its own music and a true traveler can tune up with it and equally be eco-conscious and environment-friendly while enjoying the trip. This two day trip memoir is a record of the Maheshwar visit of the two of us together carrying back some very beautiful and soulful moments.

We can take a wonderful vacation in spirit, even though we are obliged to stay at home, if we will only drop our burdens from our minds for a while. But no amount of travel will give us rest and recreation if we carry our work and worries with us.

Laura Ingalls Wilder

A travel trip makes sense only if we are completely free of all burdens. It was the summer vacation of 2018 when I visited Maheshwar, a small town situated on the banks of Narbada river in Khargone district of Madhya Pradesh, around ninety kilometers from Indore. It was not a planned tour, but a sudden and spontaneous urge to move out leisurely and go to some other place which would provide calm and balm, a real holiday and a break from the daily humdrums.

To travel is to explore, to delve into the surroundings, to enjoy every step and pathways, to absorb the nature and landscape, to mark the forests and rocks, to interact with the natives, to speak like them, to discover their local and regional aspects –food, clothing and living. This is what my travel companion, my life companion Ravi taught me since I took the first step of our journey together. His passion for travel is very stimulating and it is he who has developed a new vision, a philosophy of travel and has transformed my perception about travelling. For me, travel trip was limited to visiting a place for a change and amusement – to have some restful moments away from the daily monotonous routine. But now I have a new insight – I feel the travel, I try to explore and discover the historical significance of the places we pass through, observe the cultural traits and of course taste the local cuisine. The art, history and architecture besides the natural beauty, the forestry, vegetation, agriculture, occupation all have become part of my interest and I carry the memories with every trip which now has a very vast canvas. I owe a lot to Ravi for this insight and have now realised that besides these physical and natural enchantments the metaphysical and mythological inclinations are also to be lived. The ambience and the vibrations of a track or destination is what make a difference when we are in a journey. Sometimes it is very positive and elevating; at times it can be eerie and depleting.

Before I actually recollect and narrate my trip to Maheshwar I would like to acknowledge that the idea emerged from the suggestion of my sister Sarita, with whom I shared the memories and she said why don't you write a memoir on this trip and it struck me right. The selection of the destination was obviously done by Ravi because as I mentioned earlier that it was a spontaneous decision. Ravi is particular in his choice as per the time, the climate, the requirement and the mood. He wished to move to a lesser known and less crowded place somewhere in plains because our earlier tours have been in the hills. So he searched casually on Google and suggested Maheshwar, to which I readily agreed. We packed the same day we planned the trip and here I would like to mention again that Ravi taught me to travel light. With little luggage he feels free and one backpack is sufficient for him. It was initially difficult for me to pack and I would keep fumbling keeping and removing things very seriously but like a true traveler Ravi would get ready with a few necessary things and would look at me amusingly –teasing and frowning and, after a few trips with him I have learnt to pack according to the desired destination and climate. He knew that I would purchase the local articles from the places we would visit so the luggage would increase when we return. Light luggage makes us feel light and things required can be purchased on the way.

It was the last week of June when we started from Chittorgarh early morning around five. I would feel little lazy in getting up so early but Ravi is an early riser and very punctual too. So I have to be cautious when I have to move out with him. The weather gave us a very beautiful treat – it started drizzling as it was almost the advent of monsoon. We started by our car and the drive itself was very pleasant and the journey very alluring. Early morning devotional hymns filled us with pure vibrations and the golden sunrays set in from the car mirror and filled us with positive energy. Around eight we halted for breakfast. We had potato stuffed paratha which was much required because we felt that heavy breakfast was necessary as we started quite early in the morning and it would be almost post lunch time while we reach Maheshwar. After hot tea we felt nice and started our journey afresh.

Maheshwar is about 375 kilometers from Chittorgarh. We passed through the greens and browns of the route. While entering Madhya Pradesh we noticed farmlands, big trees and ample greenery on both sides of the highway. It was a smooth drive, melodious songs kept us musing and we reached our desired destination even before we had expected. We definitely were exhausted but at the same time very happy. The first priority was to look for our stay arrangements. After talking and enquiring about the required place we strolled in the small town and with the very first interaction with the natives we discerned that they were very helping and innocent folk. We screened a few hotels, we prefer to look to the surroundings and the place ourselves hence we avoid booking online especially at places where we are sure we would not face any difficulty. After a short search we finally settled at a hotel which had presentable facilities along with green surrounding. The room was spacious with large windows and the backyard had open space with lots of large trees making the whole stay very calm and soothing. We settled down, had lunch and since Ravi had driven about four hundred kilometers by now, obviously he was tired and needed some rest.

By five in the evening we moved out towards the famous fort at the banks of Narbada River. A magnificent piece of Maratha architecture, it was once the palace of Rani Ahilya Bai Holkar, the queen of Malwa and is popularly recognised as the Queen's Fort. It was built in ancient times, then subsequently by the Mughals and then reconstructed in the eighteenth century by Rani Ahilya Bai. It had been the axis of Maratha regime in those times as the queen had shifted her administrative center from Indore to Maheshwar and even today it proudly pronounces its historical significance. The whole complex is designed on a hill beside the river along with temples and cenotaphs. The fort now is used as a Hotel and a part of it has been retained as tourist attraction. Prince Richard Holkar the queen's descendant and son of the last king of Indore converted his home in Ahilya Wada into a guest residence and has restored it as Ahilya Fort Hotel and it is now a fusion of history and hospitality. A big statue of Rani Ahilya Bai is installed here in which she is holding a Shivling in her hands. It is said that the Queen was a devotee of Lord Shiva. This place is known as Ahilya Wada. The Shivling Puja is still performed by the Brahmins on the Ghats of the river as a ritual. A large Bilwa tree, the leaves of which are offered to Lord Shiva is very auspicious and exclusive here, because it has a nine leaves bunch instead of three leaves string. This attracts everybody and the devotees are filled with blissful experience and enchantment at this place. The southern entrance of the fort has a flight of steps and a massive arched gateway. It has a panoramic view from the banks of the sacred river. The edifice well defines the needs of warfare and defense and beholds its strategic importance. Another entrance is through the road of the town. The whole structure is a fine example of fort architecture. Architects Bhujdar and Gajdar renovated it and a combination of Rajasthan artwork was infused introducing arches, oriel windows and jharokhas in its basic design. The cenotaphs of the Holkar family are spectacular; especially the cenotaph of Queen Ahilya Bai is very remarkable and is popularly known as Ahilyeshwar Shivalaya because it enfolds a Shivlinga. This construction is in Nagar style and the black curvilinear tower of the cenotaph has a brass finial. In all, the entire fort is an architectural masterpiece. We were fascinated while exploring the different parts and corners of the fort which seemed to boast proudly of its grandiose and heritage. It took us one more visit the next day to explore and feel the majesty and class of the fort. But before it turned dark we had enough time to sit back on the Ghats and watch the activities of the visitors. It was a very relaxing evening – the lush green riverfront and scenic beauty was captivating. Boats, ships and streamers ferried the tourists and we too had a boat ride – the gentle breeze blew and swayed us across the clear stream – it was a memorable and amazing sail. The scenic beauty around the banks of the river on all sides was strikingly beholding. And yes, the real time for Ravi to fulfill his passion for photography. I would like to mention here that unlike other tourists who are simply busy capturing their own photographs, Ravi is deeply interested in nature and spot photography. He has the sense to capture those exclusive and breathtaking pictures which we retain as special memories. And when we come back and friends and family wish to see our photographs, we have very few, but we have exquisite pictures of the landscapes and the places we go through. Only those who have similar passion for photography and love for nature would understand and appreciate our collection.

After the ride we sat down on the Ghats steps and I could see that Ravi is feeling tempted to take a dip in the holy water. There were visitors as well as natives who came in the mornings and the evenings to swim, take a dip and offer prayers in the temples. Ravi stepped down, took holy dip and enjoyed staying in water and swimming. Since I do not know swimming and am afraid of taking dip also, I retained on the bank steps simply putting my feet in the cold water which was very relaxing after the long journey. A grandfather happened to be by my side along with his two little granddaughters training them to swim and was playing with them in water. He sensed that I am afraid and at the same time I wish to take a holy dip and enjoy in the waters. He started talking to us and we came to know that he had some relatives in Chittorgarh. We felt connected as he mentioned some names with which we were also familiar. He encouraged me along with Ravi to fulfill my wish and it took a few moments for me to be in the holy stream! Though I kept hold on the chains and kept myself in a safe position, I was slightly frightened and yet I admit that it was a wonderful moment in my trip. We sat back on the steps of the river bank for quite some time. Gradually, the sun was sinking down, the calm and quiet dusk reflected shadows in the river stream, the evening sky turned silvery with the rise of crescent moon and a deep silence filled us with deeper tranquility. After some time we strolled back to our hotel and since we were tired by now we decided to rest and continue our tour the next morning.

The rising sun cast soft orange hue through the window and early morning we both moved out as we were keen to visit Sahastradhara Jalkoti, the other end of the sacred river where innumerable streams broke out and the crystal clear water produced a gleaming effect as the sun rays fell over it. The water here is not very deep and we enjoyed walking over the rocks for quite some time. Then we sat down on big rocks feeling the cold water on our feet. An unforgettable experience indeed! Thanks to the grandfather we met the day before because it was he who gave us the information about this beautiful spot and added a very pleasant morning in our short tour. We reached here by road and this place is approximately five kilometers from the town but let me admit that the spot was worth visiting – a joyous, uplifting and enthralling effect made the clear sunny day livelier and raised our spirits high. While returning back to our hotel we stopped at a tea corner for our morning tea and watched the people enjoying their morning walk. The tea in Madhya Pradesh is generally very sweet, so we would rather ask for sugar free tea and add sugar as per our taste. Mornings always bring hope and aspirations and this morning was not an exception. We could notice the flurry of activities in the town. We came back to our hotel and got ready for the second day of our tour.

Poha and Jalebi is the much relished breakfast of this state and it is equally popular in Rajasthan too, so we opted for it and the flavor of onion and lemon made it a delightful plate. Madhya Pradesh is rich in culture and heritage and has many delicacies to offer. Poha is a popular breakfast almost all over India but it is very common in this state. It is made of flattened rice and prepared in onion, curry leaves, potato and green coriander, flavored with lemon and garnished with namkeen. The street food vendors as well as the popular restaurants have jalebi in their menu, a delicacy prepared in sugar syrup. After breakfast, we moved towards the Narmada Ghats and the fort area and, the calm and peaceful atmosphere in morning was totally different from that of the previous evening. Only those who wished to take a holy dip and offer prayers were coming and performing their rituals very religiously. We visited the temples on the Ghats side, offered our prayers along with some puja material and Narmada water on the Shivling. We also offered Narmada water to the rising sun. It was a blissful moment – connecting with the Almighty at a sacred place and sitting in silence experiencing the positive vibes and energy. We spent some time on the Ghats and had the opportunity to see the fort once again. We visited Rajwada and the Jaleshwar temple dedicated to Lord Shiva. Vendors and local persons could be seen selling puja material, some articles like gems, stones, statues, shivling, rudraksha and such other things usually put up for sale at such holy sites. Few vendors earned their livelihood by selling some snacks and eatables.

Maheshwar is mentioned as Mahishmati in our ancient scriptures and literature. Mythology holds that king Sahastrarjun held Ravan prisoner for six months at this place. His temple is at the RajRajeshwar temple complex. This town is truly termed as town of temples. Our epics mention this place and its association with Sages like Jamdagni and Parshuram. Every stone of the sacred river Narbada is considered as Shankar. The Shiv temple here is a miraculous one as it has eleven lamps burning constantly since ancient times. This fire is lighted by pure ghee which the devotees contribute. These lamps have religious significance and have pure illuminating effect. It was again very entrancing to be a part of this site. The temples are all the evidence of ancient architectural skills and are centers of spiritual power and emanate pure vibrations thus enhancing the soul power of the devotees.

The art of weaving is not only an art but also the main occupation of Maheshwar. While touring we caught hold of the display of beautiful, colorful and artistic sarees everywhere in the town popularly known as Maheshwari Sarees. The patronage of royal Holkar family encouraged this art and though the fabric was originally designed for the aristocratic circle of those times and as gifts for the royal guests, today it has become popular throughout the country and business persons make it available at their outlets. Maheshwar is now a renowned weaving hub and has acquired recognition not only in India but also in other countries. The sound of looms can be heard as you pass around them. Weaving is a delicate process in which a charkha is used to weave the yarn and skilled weavers prepare very beautiful sarees with cotton as well as silk thread. We visited the looms and saw the weaving process. The Gudi Mudi workshop and the Rehwa Society Looms are the major concerns promoting this art. But these sarees are quite expensive and are mostly purchased by the affluent visitors or the foreign tourists. The common Indian visitor would prefer an affordable piece. The Tana Bana and many more shops had regular Maheshwari saree collection for visitors in a wide range. Shawls, Dress materials, Kurtas and Dupatas were also available. Like all Indian women, I am also fascinated with this decent and elegant attire. Ravi would smile as he noticed my excitement while looking at the sarees. I felt that not only these sarees looked very delicate but these were very light and lustrous. Exquisite patterns and reversible border designs made them very unique. The owner of the hotel we stayed in also owned loom and a saree shop. I purchased a few sarees and dress material from his outlet for myself as well as family and friends. It is very difficult to resist buying sarees when one is at Maheshwar and I would suggest if anyone visits this place, he or she should definitely purchase this artistic and exquisite fabric for one's collection.

The natives of the town Maheshwar are very simple. We interacted with a few people and found them very friendly and down to earth. The town has an agriculture based economy and cotton is grown here in abundance besides the food grains. The clothing and living is simple village style but the town has now emerged as a tourist destination and hence a lot of hotels and restaurants had been constructed and business activity has gained much importance. We had the preparations of paneer, dal, seasonal vegetables and chapatti along with rice pulao for our meals and, yes dessert made our dinner delicious. Sweets of numerous variety is a prominent part of Madhya Pradesh plate and we noticed that the natives are quite fond of sweets and the visitors feel tempted to relish the delicacies too.

I was very keen to visit the most pristine pilgrimage, the Omkareshwar temple which is approximately an hour drive from Maheshwar. It is situated on the OM shaped island on the confluence of two sacred rivers Narbada and Kaveri and is one of the twelve Jyotirlingas in India. The Narmada River flows between Omkareshwar and Mamleshwar. Mamleshwar was originally called Amreshwar, and Mamleshwar and Omkareshwar are considered as one Jyotirlinga. We offered water, bilwa leaves and other puja material on the Shivling and were fortunate to have the Almighty's blessings. I have been an ardent devotee of Lord Shiva and it was a dream come true to be in this place today. It seemed as if we were on a pilgrimage and Lord Shiva has showered his blessings on us because as we returned we halted at Ujjain and had the fortune to visit the Mahakaal temple and the renowned Jyotirlinga. We could not resist the aspiration to visit nearby spots like the Sandeepani Ashram, the Kaal Bhairav temple and the Mangalnath temple all known for their religious and divine significance located within the purview of a few kilometers. Sandeepani Ashram was the learning place of Lord Krishna and Sudama in their childhood, a very calm and quiet place with pure vibrations and meditative influence. The Kaal Bhairav temple is also very popular where liquor is offered to the deity as part of worship which is absorbed by it. The Mangalnath temple is a wonderful shrine situated at the stretch of river Shipra. A specific ritual is performed in this temple to solve the astrological problem of the position of the Mars Planet in the horoscope. Devotees queue up to offer puja and seek blessings of Lord Shiv and Mangal planet. We halted at Mandsaur before reaching back to our home town. The Pashupati Nath temple is a very renowned cultural and religious center and has eight-faced Shiv statue as mark of rare iconography. A very artistic piece of rock carving having deep religious connotations the temple is located adjacent to Shivna River. I felt a sense of gratitude for this opportunity bestowed by the Almighty which raised our soul-consciousness and opened up new avenues and horizons for the spiritual sky. These temples and holy places are all full of miracles and mystery and hence very entrancing and mesmerising.

The way back to Chittorgarh delved both of us in a state of longingness, a sense of fulfillment yet enrapturing a vacuum, a long silence arrested us and while traveling back we were moving ahead our path feeling as if we are leaving something behind.

CHAPTER 21

Understanding Travel Writing as an Act of Cultural Translation with reference to the Travel Narrative of Nancy Prince

Dr. Alka Jhajaria

Abstract

Travel writing is a specific act of cultural translation, in which the travel writer, by representing the foreign, in effect translates it into something known by making it meaningful for a home audience. Indeed, it is a well-known truism in the study of tourism that the travel narrative is just as much a representation of the home culture of the travel writer as it is a representation of the foreign culture that the writer visits. On the basis of black writer's travelogues' study, travel writing can be understood as a genre of cultural translation as it describes traveller's interaction with white 'other'. While depicting the difference between 'self' and 'other' these travellers also reveal examples of connections and also highlights the commonalities shared between their native places and abroad where they travel. Their travel narrative demonstrates these cultural differences.

Keywords: Travel Writing, Culture, Translation, Home, Other, Nancy.

Translation studies have become more prolific and more respectable activity in recent times in the field of scholarly researches. Earlier, translation remained confined to substitution of a text of one language for a text in another. But shortly after, it began to be noticed that literary texts were constituted not primarily of language but in fact of culture, language being in effect a vehicle of culture. Translation is an act of moving or carrying across from one place or position to another, or of changing from one state of things to another. It not only applies to the languages but also to human beings because they also move across all sorts of differences and borders and in this way translated from one cultural condition to another.

Translation does not refers to complete change from one condition to other as Walter Benjamin has used the word 'tangent' in order to describe the difference between 'original' and translation. Boris Buden in an article on cultural translation cites Benjamin's views that, "translation is like a tangent which touches the circle (i.e., the original) at one single point only, thereafter to follow its own way" (quoted in Buden 200).

This idea of Benjamin is important for deconstructionist theory and out of the same deconstructionist tradition emerges the concept of cultural translation, coined by famous postcolonial theorist Homi K. Bhabha. Bhabha's concept of translation is different from traditional translation methods. This may not be confused with old fashioned sense of translation as scholars have concluded:

> What is nevertheless clear and indisputable in Bhabha's formulations of what he calls cultural translation is, firstly, that he does not at all by this term mean literary translation involving two texts from two different languages and cultures, and secondly, that what he means by translation instead is the process and condition of human migrancy. ("Cultural translation: An introduction to the problem, and Responses")

Trivedi is also critical of Bhabha and rejects this concept and suggests for use of another word in place of translation. According to him, it is not translation; it is a process of human migrancy, hence he recommends the use of other words like migration, exile or Diaspora at the place of translation.

The present paper focuses on this idea of 'cultural translation' as described by Bhabha with special reference to the travel narrative of a black woman writer. The narratives by black women demonstrate the tension involved in forms of difference between race and gender. The paper mainly refers to the autobiographical work of a black woman, Nancy Gardner Prince. It is especially difficult to find first-hand accounts written by black women because their mobility as well as their access to basic education was severely limited. Despite these difficulties Nancy Gardner Prince published her auto-biography, *A Narrative of the Life and Travels of Mrs. Nancy Prince*, in 1850.

Nancy Gardner Prince, an African-American woman was born of a free mother and seafaring father. Her maternal grandparents were slaves. During childhood Nancy and her siblings were told about the evils of slavery by her grandfather. Her father died when she was only three months old. Her mother came to Gloucester with her two children, married third husband, by whom she had six children. After her stepfather's death, her mother suffered an emotional breakdown. Nancy and her six younger siblings had to work in order to support the family. She then left home to work as a servant for white families. She recounts her experiences with the family where she serves:

> Hard labour and unkindness was too much for me; in three months, my health and strength were gone. I often looked at my employers, and thought to myself, is this your religion? I did not wonder that the girl who has lived there previous to myself, went home to die. (11)

Nancy wrote her narrative with an intention to promote a certain set of beliefs such as to improve the condition of ex-slave women and children. In her autobiography Prince frequently makes reference to her religious convictions crediting them with motivating her to do good works. Throughout the narrative, Nancy maintains the tone of a preacher. She has used her religious beliefs as a way of racial uplifting. She writes, "He made man in his own image in the image of God, created he him, male and female, that they should have dominion over the fish of the seas, the foul of the air and the beast of the field" (48). She writes that only her religious faith sustained her during years of "anxiety and toil," in which she worked to support her family. Nancy has frequently used allusions from the Bible in her narrative in order to critique the moral shortcomings of white Christians. Prince shows that although she does not approve the way white Christians teach their religion but she believes in the grace of God. Nancy changes the perception of her religious mission by removing it from one of her racist white Christian colleagues. She frankly rejects other white Christian for their attitude towards African Diaspora. In the West Indies Nancy is threatened with the loss of pay when she is offended by teaching methods of the class leader. She retorts, "I spoke to her of the necessity of being born of the spirit of God before we become members of the church of Christ, and I told her I was sorry to see the people blinded in such a way"( ). She goes to the minister and tells him that she will no longer "be guided by poor foolish women" and that "the moral conduct of the church members had been neglected."(46)." In this way Nancy separates herself from the white clergymen of the time who according to her had issues of classism, colonialism and racism.

Nancy also presents the concept of womanhood. Her childhood presents the sad stories of pathos but if we compare her with other women characters in the narrative such as Nancy's mother and sister she appears as a strong and independent woman who saves her younger sister from a brothel. Nancy wanted to encourage the role of women in society at that time but she was frustrated to see their inefficiency. She feels a sense of superiority towards other African American women who she thinks as foolish or not conducting themselves properly. "Prince made a conscious attempt to oppose the multiplicity of negative stereotypes and myths circulating about African American women, particularly freeborn" (Moody 77).

In 1824 Nancy's life changed dramatically when she married Nero Prince and moved with him to Russia. They came to Copenhagen, where they stayed for twelve days. They visited the King's palace and other beautiful buildings of the city and attended a number of entertainments among the Danes and English. Nancy finds that their custom and manners are similar. Unlike her previous experiences, she finds that these people are "very attentive to strangers" (15). The languages spoken here are Dutch, French and English. With her sweet experiences Nancy and her husband come to their destination St Petersburg. Here also they are welcomed from all quarters as Nancy recounts her experience, "There I spent six weeks very pleasantly, visiting and receiving friends, after the manner of the country" (15). She notices the cultural difference between her religion and the religion of the people where she visited. She could not participate in the various amusements of the parties of these people due to cultural differences. She writes, "I told them my religion did not allow of dancing or dice playing, which formed part of the amusement" (16). But, "translation is the performative nature of cultural communication" (Bhabha 228). Nancy finds that these people were very strict in their religion and indulged her in the same activities. Nancy was able to cope up with these cultural differences and thankful to God for this. "By the help of God I was ever enabled to maintain my stand" (26). In Russia there was no prejudice against colour. she finds, "there were there all castes, and the people of all nations, each in their place and it is well known that the colour of one's skin does not prohibit from any place or station that he or she may be capable of occupying" (16). In Russia, "all religion is tolerated, but the native Russians are subject to the Greek Church. There are number of institutions in St Petersburg where children of all classes have the privilege of instruction" (36). Here Nancy observes the people of different classes. The village houses built of logs are resided by the peasants. These people till the soil and most of them are slaves and are much degraded" (38). Nancy finds, "the rich own the poor, but they are not suffered to separate families or sell them off the soil" (38). The common language is a mixture of Slavonian and Polish. Prince boarded children, and, having learned to sew, started a business making clothing for infants and toddlers, which she sold to the nobility. these dresses were handsomely wrought in French and English styles. The nobility make use of Modern Greek, French and English. She writes, "I learned the languages in six months, so as to be able to attend to my business and also made some proficiency in the French" (38). In Russia, Active in the local Protestant church, she also helped establish an orphanage in St. Petersburg and distributed Bibles at the royal palace. In 1833, after ten years in St. Petersburg, Prince returned to the United States for reasons of health. Returning to Boston, she finds that everything is in confusion but she is thankful to God for guiding her in such a way that she was capable of helping her fellow brethren whose circumstances were similar to her own as she writes

> I found many a poor little orphan destitute and afflicted, and on account of colour shut out from all the asylums for poor children. At this my heart was moved, and I proposed to my friends the necessity of a home for such, where they might be sheltered from contaminating evils that beset their path. (41)

She laid the plan for this purpose in a meeting of the people because she had an experience of assisting this type of asylum in St Petersburg. She began with eight children. A board of seven females and a committee of twelve gentlemen were created but due to the lack of funds it could not succeed. In Boston Nancy attended Anti-slavery society established by

W. L. Garrison, "Their design was the amelioration of nominally free coloured people of these states and the emancipation of the slaves in other states" (42). In November 1840, she left for Jamaica to raise up and encourage the emancipated inhabitants and teach the young children to read and work.

Nancy could not tolerate oppression in any form. In Jamaica when she stays in the house of one of the class leaders, she was warned by the authority for not following their methods. In this concern she writes, "I spoke to her of the necessity of being born of the spirit of God before we become members of the church of Christ, and told her I was sorry to see the people blinded in such a way" (46). When this matter comes to the minister, she tells him that she did not come there to be "guided by a poor foolish woman" (46).

Nancy is disillusioned after meeting the American consul. She writes, "he told me he was very glad to see me for such a purpose as I had in view in visiting Jamaica, but he said it was a folly for the Americans to come to the island to better their condition; he said they came to him everyday praying him to send them home" (48). Nancy attended the Baptist Missionary meeting in Queen Street Chapel. She notices, "there was but one coloured minister on the platform" (48). It is generally the policy of these missionaries to have the sanction of coloured ministers, "The coloured people give more readily, and are less suspicious of imposition, if one from themselves recommends the measure. This, the missionaries understand very well, and know how to take advantage of it." (49)

Nancy visits the market and feels about the coloured people, "it may be hoped they are not stupid set of beings they have been called; here surely we see industry; they are enterprising and quick in their perceptions, determined to possess themselves, and to possess property besides, and quite able to take care of themselves" (50). These people wanted to know why Nancy was so inquisitive about them. She told them, "We had heard in America that you are lazy, and that emancipation has been of no benefit to you; I wish to inform myself of the truth respecting you, and give a true account of my return" (50). These people were very happy and heartly thanked Nancy. But when she goes to the East Market, she finds there people from different nations. She feels, "the Jews and Spanish looked at me very black". (50)

This autobiographical work presents the socio-cultural and historical account of the places visited by Nancy Prince. Dictionary of Literary Biography on Nancy Gardner Prince states, "By observing and experiencing the social and economic climates of nineteenth-century Russia, the British-controlled West Indies, and several parts of the United States, including the South, Prince came to view racism, sexism, poverty, and political struggle as universal problems and not peculiar to any one country or race of people." Prince brought her 'Americanism' and 'black womanhood' with her wherever she went, as a result, neither she nor the places she visited could be entirely free from racial, gendered, or class-based hierarchies.

In Boston she worked as a seamstress, abolitionist and lecturer on Russia. In 1840 and 1842 Prince travelled to Jamaica as a Christian missionary. She was well respected in her time as a social activist and writer who made astute observations on the social and economic climate of Russia, the West Indies and parts of the South in the nineteenth-century. At every place, she struggles to create a "home" for herself and others through discourses of race, class, gender, and empire. Returning to Boston, she established an institution for homeless children of colour, but it closed after three months due to lack of funding. Later, she joined a mission of a Reverend Ingraham to assist the newly emancipated slaves in Kingston, Jamaica. Nancy finds that most of the people of Jamaica are emancipated slaves. Their condition after abolition of slavery is also not very satisfactory as she sees "every advantage is taken of their ignorance, the same spirit of cruelty is opposed to them that held them for centuries in bondage" (53). But if compared to slavery their present state is better.

Nancy established a school for poor destitute girls modelled on Mico institute. She formed a society of forty people who will contribute three dollars per year. For collecting funds for free Labor school in Jamaica she comes to Boston but could not collect required sum. She took fifty dollars from her own purse and returned to Jamaica but finds everything has been changed. "The people were in a state of agitation, several were changed, and insurrection was so great that it was found necessary to increase the army to quell it. It was not safe to be there (57)." She left Jamaica for New York. She also notices the dilemma of freed slaves. "It is well known that those that were freed knowing their children were still in bondage, were not satisfied." (58)

The year 1838 brought a change in the scenario. The general freedom throughout the British islands gave the death blow to the power of the master. Mothers received their "emancipated children with joy and they no longer looked the picture of despair, fearing to see their mulatto son or daughter beating or abusing their younger brothers and sisters of a darker skin" (58). Nancy regards herself as superior to black persons from outside of the US. In this regard, "Prince's narrative employs the same tone of colonial arrogance similar to her contemporary Anglo-American missionaries."

Nancy Prince's Narrative can be called a psychological travel book as it deals with the journey inward as well as outward. The binary opposition of self and other creates the increasing consciousness of cultural differences. Here travel writing is understood as a process of cultural translation where the traveller is interacting with the foreign culture and trying to make sense of it. Thus, Nancy Gardner Prince in her travel narrative has presented as an implicit story about the self by the process of cultural changing.

References

Bhabha, Homi. *Location of Culture.* London: Routledge, 1994.

Boris Buden, Stefan Nowotny, Sherry Simon, Ashok Bery & Michael Cronin (2009) Cultural translation: An introduction to the problem, and Responses, Translation Studies, 2:2, 196-219. Web https://doi.org/10.1080/14781700902937730

Ferguson, Moira. *Nine Black Women: An Anthology of Nineteenth-Century Writers from The United States, Canada, Bermuda and Caribbean.* New York: Routledge, 1998.

Gambier, *Yves and Luc van Doorslaer eds.* Handbook of Translation Studies. Vol 2. John

Benjamins Publishing Company, 2011. *ProQuest Ebook Central.* Accessed on 16-08-2019

<http://ebookcentral.proquest.com/lib/britishcouncilonline >

Kenny Gale L. *Contentious Liberties: American Abolitionists in Post-Emancipation Jamaica.* Athens, Georgia: University of Georgia Press, 2010.

Prince, Nancy Gardner. *A Narrative of Life and Travels* by Mrs. Nancy Gardner Prince. Boston, 1853.

Trivedi, Harish. (2005). "Translating Culture vs. Cultural Translation" in 91 st Meridian, Volume 4, No. 1. accessible at https://iwp.uiowa.edu/91st/vol4-num1. 4.1 spring 2005 https://iwp.uiowa.edu/91st/vol4-num1/translating-culture-vs-cultural-translation web 24/8/2019

"Women in World History: A Biographical Encyclopedia. Encyclopedia.com. 13 Aug. 2019 <https://www.encyclopedia.com>.

Yee, Shirley J. *Black Women Abolitionists: A Study in Activism,* 1828-1860. Knoxville: University of Tennessee Press, 1992.

List of Contributors

1. **Dr. Anita Luther Bhasin**, Asst. Prof. KES Shroff College, Kandivali (W), Mumbai.
2. **Dr. Anoopama Yadav**, Assistant Professor of English, Maharaja Aggrasen PG College for Women, Jhajjar, Haryana.
3. **Dr. Atiqa Kelsy**, Associate Professor, Department of English St Xavier's College, Jaipur.
4. **Anshuman Singh Chauhan**, Director, APJ, SAP Labs India Pvt. Ltd.
5. **Dr. Alka Jhajhria**, Assistant Professor, English, Dr Bhim Rao Ambedkar, Government College, Sri Ganganagar.
6. **Mrs. Anita John**, Department of Political Science, Mayo College Girls' School, Ajmer.
7. **Ambika Gahlot**, Assistant Professor, English, Shri Ratanlal Kanwarlal Patni Girls' College, Kishangarh, Rajasthan.
8. **Anant Pandey**, Automotive Journalist, Motoroids, Mumbai, Maharashtra.
9. **Dr. Gargi Singh**, PGT Psychology, Mayo College Girls' School, Ajmer.
10. **Guman Singh Gehlot**, Assistant Professor, English, Government College Raipur (Pali, Rajasthan).
11. **Dr. Jyoti Sareen**, Associate Professor, English, Government College, Chhattargarh, Bikaner.
12. **Karthika V.P.**, Assistant Professor, Department of English, Government College, Daman.
13. **Dr. Kirandeep** Associate Professor, English, Ch. Balluram Godara Govt. Girls' College, Sriganganagar (Rajasthan).
14. **Dr. Mamta Chanwaria**, Associate Professor, Department of Political Science, M.L.V. Government College, Bhilwara.
15. **Dr. Prerna Maheshwari**, Associate Professor, Department of History, Government Dungar College, Bikaner.

16. **Dr. Rashmi Bhatnagar**, Associate Professor, Government College, Pushkar (Rajasthan).

17. **Dr Ranjit Kaur**, Assistant Professor, Department of English, St Xavier's College, Jaipur.

18. **Dr. Sanjana Sharma**, Associate Professor, Department of English, S.P.C. Government College, Ajmer.

19. **Dr. Tanuja Yadav**, Associate Professor, Department of Languages, Manipal University Jaipur.

20. **Dr. Urvashi Sabu**, Associate Professor, Dept of English PGDAV College, Delhi University, Delhi.

21. **Dr. Yashoda Verma**, Assistant Professor, Department of Languages, Manipal University Jaipur.

Index